A wide range of Christian books is available from EP. If you would like a free catalogue please write to us or contact us by e-mail. Alternatively, you can view the whole catalogue online at one of our websites.

EP Books
Faverdale North, Darlington, DL3 0PH, England

e-mail: sales@epbooks.org
web: www.epbooks.org

EP Books USA
P. O. Box 614, Carlisle, PA 17013, USA

e-mail: usasales@epbooks.org
web: www.epbooks.us

Sales of our books help to promote the missionary work of EP in making good Christian literature available at affordable prices in poorer countries of the world and training pastors and preachers to teach God's Word to others.

Sufism Lecture Series

SUFISM LECTURE SERIES

SUFISM
SUFISM AND PEACE
SUFISM AND KNOWLEDGE
SUFISM AND WISDOM
SUFISM AND ISLAM

HAZRAT SALAHEDDIN ALI NADER ANGHA
PIR OVEYSSI

MTO PUBLICATIONS ®

Nader Angha
Sufism Lecture Series

ISBN 978-190491661-1

A catalogue record for this book is available from the British Library.
Published in Great Britain in 2011 by MTO Publications ®.
Printed in China by R.R.Donnelley

www.mto.org

Contents

Wherever the masculine gender is used, it is solely for the purpose of linguistic convenience. Since the intent of religion is for the spiritual elevation of each individual, we believe that religion addresses the soul, and the soul is not subject to gender classification.

INTRODUCTION

A few years ago Hazrat Pir began one of his lectures by asking the audience these questions, "If there were only one in the world, and that one were you, what would be your name? Who would you be? Would you hate? Would you love?" Only an instant lapsed before he calmly asked, "If there were one, and that one had all the knowledge of the universe, and could respond to all your needs and all your wants, what would you do?" Then he said, Sufism is about this "ONE".

Hazrat Pir's method of teaching is definitely thought provoking, and his students say demanding and challenging. Some say he evokes the same system of learning as Socrates did with his students. Those who have interviewed him usually confess that they are totally disarmed by his questions, becoming engaged in an intense learning experience. True to his mission, Hazrat Pir never ceases to teach. His main goal is to show people how they may attain the true state of human dignity, peace and tranquility. His definition of the human being rises above social, cultural and psychological definitions.

Sophisticated communication systems have linked people worldwide, breaking down the "absolutes" that societies, communities and countries had defined and kept sacred for themselves. It is the age of relativity. While exposure to diversity has expanded people's vision of the world, it has also brought elements of insecurity and instability into the day-to-day life of many people. When standards collapse and values shift, where can we find the ultimate definition of our "self"?

Hazrat Pir says, "Each person is a complex and unique masterpiece." Most of us , if not all, would like this statement to be true. But what prevents us from experiencing it? What must occur for us to approach the understanding of the magnitude of this statement? If we don't allow our imagination to quickly define it, package it and file it away, we could start on an intense journey of self-realization. This journey would change the entire fabric of societies, human interactions and legal and social systems. It involves moving through the multidimensional patterns of the social conditionings that have structured our lives, formed our identities, personalities, self-worth. Even our perceptions of others and our value systems would be affected. How can we put these aside? And if we should put them aside, then what would be the yardstick with which we could measure our achievements, our knowledge and our understanding of anything?

Hazrat Pir says, "You are the measure for everything." He is often heard saying, "You have everything that you need. All you need to do is to release the boundaries you have created, then 'reality' will unveil." But if one wants to be this "unique masterpiece", how, realistically, does one "release the boundaries?"

"Know thyself," wrote the philosopher Plato about integrity; because "an unexamined life is not worth living." From the time of the Greeks, Western philosophy has advocated self-knowledge or internal learning. This internal learning is at the heart of Islam. As the Holy Prophet Mohammad has said, "Whoever knows the true self knows God."

To begin at the beginning - know thyself. The "i", the individual, is a cherished concept, the acknowledged foundation upon which democracy is built. By transforming the "i", one can go a long way towards transforming the greater world in which the "i" lives. The belief in the perfectibility of the Self has strengthened the fiber of Western society and the collapse of this belief in the twentieth century has brought about alienation and uncertainty in modern societies. Untouched by today's social, economic and political shifts, Hazrat Pir represents a strong and clear voice, reminding us of the urgency to know the true and stable "I". In so doing, he reaffirms the human being's capacity to master the self.

One of the significant contributions of Hazrat Pir to the reservoir of world knowledge is the concept that, because the world has projected its divisions and boundaries onto the vulnerable "i", one must create a process for achieving mastery of mind. This is done by first removing these divisions and boundaries imposed upon the "i" through an inner experience of religion. It begins with spiritual integration and ends with a complete metamorphosis. It is no coincidence that two of the healthiest and strongest mystical minds of the Catholic tradition - St. John of the Cross and St. Teresa of Avila - learned much about their mystical journey from Islam as it was received into the Spanish Moorish tradition.

Much can be learned from the way Hazrat Pir teaches. Ideally, a student should think: "I will commit myself not to the idea but the process of mastering my own mind. If enough of us do the same 'the world' will simultaneously change because 'the world' is us." This is a simple way of stating a complicated process, but it is a beginning.

This series of essays, scripts of lectures given by Hazrat Pir discuss his teaching as it relates to the history of Sufism, peace, wisdom, knowledge, healing, meditation, love, prayer, balance, and alchemy. The author, Hazrat Pir Molana Salaheddin Ali Nader Shah Angha, is the forty-second master of Maktab Tarighat Oveyssi Shahmaghsoudi (School of Islamic Sufism). This school traces its lineage back to the very advent of Islam in the seventh century A.D. While Hazrat Pir's lectures are faithful to the tradition which produced him and which he now guides, they also reflect the mark he has made on that tradition. Raised and trained in the esoteric tradition of Sufism and educated in the West, Hazrat Pir is exceptionally sensitive to the modern world. Accomplished in the disciplines of religion, science, philosophy and poetry, and trained by his father, Molana Hazrat Shah Maghsoud Sadegh Angha (Professor Angha), who was a great master of Sufism and an advanced physicist, Hazrat Pir has, from a very young age developed not only a perceptive and accomplished mind, but also an expansive spirit.

Our desire to transform the world, he teaches, must begin with a transformation of "i" into "I", the true Self. To the Sufi, this necessitates a dialogue between heart and mind. What Westerners call internal learning, or self-knowledge is, to the Sufi, more like a glorified "i" short of a transformation into Self. For example, Hazrat Pir teaches that drug addiction, the scourge of modern society, will elude well-meaning people's attempts to eradicate it, until they understand how to heal the mind of the addiction, and discover the stable "I'. To heal the mind of its addiction, one must acknowledge that God, and not the ego is at the center of the "I". Only then is one capable of living a healthy and balanced life.

An examination of Hazrat Pir's example would result in a welcoming of a scientific understanding of the mind that will complement the existing one in the West. Islam is much in the news these days and concerned people want to know more about a culture that is at once alien and familiar – as familiar as the lines from the *Holy Qur'an*, "I am closer to you than your jugular vein." Most Westerners would not have ever read these words unless they were familiar with a poem of the same name by French writer James Sacré. Yet there is a certain basic sanity about those words rooted in a deeper source than that of the creative ego. As heirs of the Greek tradition, the West is only beginning to realize why the heart of Islam seems so familiar - it has always been there, part of its world, part of its culture, part of its "I" from the beginning.

So it seems fitting that on American soil, a nation founded on the spirit of exploration and discovery, Hazrat Pir has designed and built a memorial in memory of his teacher and father, Professor Angha. In three dimensions, near Novato, California stands a wonderful metaphor for 1400 years of spiritual labor and the integration of the human being's consciousness. There in architecture and here in words on the page, Hazrat Pir encourages the seeker to submit to his or her own metamorphosis and flower like the art of the memorial through the integration of Self, through integrity to the final union with God.

SUFISM

He is the truth, He is the Exalted

"Hope is planted seed in fertile ground that bears fruit.
In the land of my heart the plant of despair never grows."

The Secret Word

You may ask, "What relevance does this have to Sufism?" The above words may seem poetical, but they constitute the essence of Sufi teachings. Before explaining this, it may be of interest to you to know some of the theories presented by scholars as to the origin of Sufism.

From one perspective we can say that Sufism dates as far back as the first human being who cognized God. On the other hand, we can say that Sufism is Islam. I will explain both perspectives as we move along.

Sufism is the essence of the Prophets' teachings. It is the Way of the Prophets. It has existed since the beginning of human history, for its seed lies within every human heart. In each age, God has sent Prophets to lead people to the knowledge of the "Him" – Zoroaster, Moses, Buddha, Jesus, David, Mohammad – to name

a few. Each Prophet has brought humanity a unique instruction
to be learned and mastered in order to progress on the inward
journey toward "God". The great ninth century Sufi, Bayazid
Bastami, described the history of Sufism by stating, "Its seeds were
set at the time of Adam, they sprouted under Noah and flowered
under Abraham. Grapes formed at the time of Moses, and they
ripened at the time of Jesus. In the time of Mohammad, they were
made into pure wine."[1]

The following is a summary of the various theories presented by
scholars about the origins of Sufism. Some sources relate Sufism's
origins as having been influenced by the Hindu Fakirs, relating
the ascetic practices of the Fakirs to that of the Sufis.[2] Others see it
as an outgrowth of Buddhism, because of the similarities found in
some of the customs of the Sufis and Buddhist sects, as well as the
extensive use of visions in both.[3] They also find similarity in the
lives of the Buddha and one of the renowned Sufi Masters, Ibrahim
Adham. They were both princes who left everything behind in
order to find the Absolute. The Japanese scholar Toshihiko Izutsu
endeavored to show similarities between Buddhism and other Far
Eastern beliefs and practices, such as the link between Taoism, and

Sufism.[4]

Others trace the roots of Sufism to Christianity,[5] seeing similarities between the austerity of the Syrian monks and that of the Sufis. While both Christian monks and Sufis have sought to distance themselves from superficial attractions of the world, there is an important difference in attitude between the two. Whereas the Christian monks withdrew into monasteries to avoid temptation, the Sufis did not need to abandon the world in such a physical sense; it was their practice to overcome their worldly desires so that their physical environment would have no influence upon them. As my grandfather, Hazrat Mir Ghotbeddin Mohammad Angha has said, "Be among people, but do not partake of their bad habits." And the Holy Prophet Mohammad (peace and blessings upon him) has said, "People are like stones brought to shore. It is when they brush against each other that their sharp edges are smoothed out." Furthermore, the *Holy Qur'an (57:27)* explicitly states that there should be no monasticism in Islam: "But the monasticism which they invented for themselves, We did not prescribe for them."

Quite a few British scholars have said that Sufism was influenced by Neo-Platonism. The flaw in this statement will become evident as I explain Sufism. Others argue that Islam began in an area where both ancient Oriental and Christian influences were great, thereby influencing Islam from its onset. These theories first of all show how little these scholars know about the reality of religion, and second, the entire concept of revelation upon which Islam is founded is denied. Social, cultural, ethnic and tribal influences which shape and form religion by the hands of people are mistaken for the genuine message of religion.

Sufism is generally accepted to be the mystical dimension of Islam. Hujwiri,[6] in the 11th century, presented several views of the origin of the term, "Sufi." Some scholars said that Sufism is derived from the word *ahl-suffa* – the people of the Bench – which refers to the platform on which the Holy Prophet Mohammad and the believers used to sit while worshipping God. Others say that they were named Sufis because of their habit of wearing *suf* (wool). The habit of wearing wool next to the skin dates back to the first masters of Islamic Sufism. But while this theory of the derivation of the word does have a foundation in the practices of Sufism, the words of Hazrat Mir Ghotbeddin Mohammad Angha clarifies this point: "While every Sufi wears wool, not every person who wears wool – *suf* – is a Sufi." And yet others have concluded that Sufis were named Sufis because of the *safa* – purity – of their hearts and the cleanliness of their actions. Therefore, the practitioners of *safa* are called Sufis, meaning "pure-hearted." What historians have eluded to is not incorrect, but is incomplete. They have presented the outer form of Sufism, while its inner meaning has been beyond their personal experience.

If we look closely at the last three hypotheses we will note that to be called a Sufi had certain requirements. To be a companion of the Prophet surely requires a different mode of action and behavior. It also requires purity of heart, spiritual awareness, and sacredness of goal. In essence, the People of the Bench, or the companions of the Holy Prophet, must have been aware of the significance of the teachings of the Holy Prophet, and must have been intent on being trained by him, because they wanted to know God. Thus, if wearing wool was one of the conditions, they did so. Wearing wool was a mere reminder not to surrender to earthly absorptions. The aim was to reach a state of purity, through which they would be in direct relationship with God, unite with God, be annihilated in God – as the Holy Prophet had declared, *la-ilaha-illa'llah*. Reaching this state means that no other but God is in one's heart – *safa*.

This method of purification through submission to God, and annihilation in God was termed *ma'rifa*, meaning acquaintance and cognition. If we want to be exact, the actual word for Sufism is *Irfan*, derived from the word *ma'rifa*. Cognition refers to a state whereby nothing remains unknown to us about the subject of inquiry. In this context it refers to the cognition of oneself and therefore cognition of God. The one who teaches this method of cognition is known as the *arif* – he who has attained the most exalted state of existence through annihilation and permanence in God. The esoteric wisdom of cognition was transmitted from the Holy Prophet to his cousin and son in-law Ali ibn Abu Talib known as Amir al-Mo'menin (peace be upon him). With the assassination of Imam Ali (pbuh), the Umayyads came to power, a dynasty whose members were known for their worldliness and impious behavior.

However, the sanctity of the message of Islam and the tradition of the Holy Prophet were kept intact through an unbroken chain of transmission by the great masters of Maktab Tarighat Oveyssi Shahmaghsoudi. While mainstream Islam fell into the hands of the clerics and jurists, these masters passed on the inner message of Islam through their teachings, writings, and students. Islam would not have survived had it not been for the selfless sacrifice of these great spiritual leaders.

The name Oveyssi School is due to a renowned master Oveys Gharani (Uways al-Qarani), whose way of inward cognition was confirmed by the Holy Prophet Mohammad. Therefore, I will start the chronological history of this School with a brief biography of him. Hazrat Oveys Gharani was born in a village called Gharan, close to Najd in Yemen. He was killed in the war of Saffeyn led by Imam Ali, in the year 37/657. Ibn Batoute, the historian, has mentioned of his tomb being located in Damascus. It is recorded that the Holy Prophet would face Yemen and say: "The breath of the Merciful comes to me from Yemen."[7] The Holy Prophet had his Cloak sent to Hazrat Oveys, an event signifying his holy dignity. Hazrat Oveys' way of cognition was confirmed as the Holy Prophet Mohammad said: "Follow the way of Oveys." , and "He is the pre-emptor of my genus." Hazrat Oveys' famous aphorism is, "Keep thy heart."

One of the first to be initiated into the Sufi tradition was a Persian man from Isfahan called Rouzbeh, son of Khoshnoudan, who was related to King Manuchehr. A Zoroastrian who had converted to Christianity, and when he met the Holy Prophet in the city of Medina, he became a Muslim. He became famous as Salman Farsi, and holds a high position in the history of Islam. The Prophet of Islam called him a member of his own family. Salman's passing occurred in 36/656, and his tomb is by the Tigris River in Baghdad, Iraq.

After Hazrat Oveys and Salman Farsi, Hazrat Habib ibn Salim Ra'i took on the necessary task of leading the people to the right course and gave the disciples instructions in Islam through the inward method of cognition. His successor was Hazrat Soltan Ebrahim Adham, a prince from Balkh who gave up his reign for the path of worship and self-discipline. Trained in the discipline of Sufism by Hazrat Habib ibn Ra'i, he also served Imam Mohammad Bagher (pbuh), the fifth Imam of the shi'a. The existing Sufi orders of Adhamieh and Choshtieh (Chisti) in India are traced back to him. The year of his passing is recorded as 160/776.

The successor of Ibrahim Adham was Hazrat Abu Ali Shaqiq al-Balkhi, who served as companion to Imam Moussa Kazem (pbuh), the seventh Imam of the Shi'a. According to some sources he was martyred for being a Shi'a in 154/770 or 174/790. His successor was Hazrat Sheikh Abu Torab Nakhshabi, who was a nobleman of Khorasan, known for his asceticism. He trained such eminent devotees as Abi Amr al-Istakhri and Abu Abdollah Jalai. He was followed by Hazrat Sheikh Abi Amr al-Istakhri, who passed away about 300/912; and then Hazrat Abu Ja'far Hazza, who succeeded him during the era of the Deylamian dynasty in Shiraz. He is one of the eminent masters of the School. He passed away in 341/950, and his tomb is located in Shiraz, Iran.

Hazrat Sheikh Kabir Abu Abdollah Mohammad-ibn Khafif Shirazi was the next in the line of succession. This great master of the School, who lived during the 4th/11th century, developed a special method of training, now known as Khafifieh Oveyssieh. He was followed by Hazrat Sheikh Hossein Akkar, whose full name was Hossein ibn Mohammad al- Houri al-Firouzabadi. He guided many on the path of self-knowledge, including an eminent devotee named Sheikh Morshed Abu-Isshaq Shahriar Kazerouni, who became his successor. He attained the highest state of cognition in Sufism, passed away in 391/1000, and is entombed in Shiraz.

Sheikh Morshed Abu-Isshaq Shahriar Kazerouni was born in

Navard, a village of Kazeroun, in 356/966. He was a contemporary of al-Ghader Bellah, an Abassid Caliph. His training began at the age of 15, and he attained the highest state of cognition and was given the Holy Cloak at the age of twenty. Because of his well-known efforts to propagate Islamic Sufism, he was also called Sheikh the Judge. He passed away in 426/1034 in Kazeroun, and was buried in Ganjabad.

His successor was Hazrat Khatib Abolfath Abdolkarim, known as a scientist, who passed away in 442/1050. He was followed by Hazrat Ali-ibn Hassan Basri, who spent most of his life in Egypt. His successor was Hazrat Serajeddin Abolfath Mahmoud-ibn Mahmoudi Sabouni Beyzavi. Born in Baghdad in 500/1106, he traveled to Damascus and then to Egypt, where he was received by King Najmeddin Ayub, father of Salaheddin. He remained in Egypt until the end of his life. He trained his successor Hazrat Sheikh Abu Abdollah Rouzbehan Baghli Shirazi, who is considered one of the most illustrious masters of Sufism. Of the many books he wrote, *Fidele D'Amour* is best known in the West. He passed away in 606/1209, and his tomb is located in Shiraz, Iran, in a district called Gate of the Sheikh.

He was succeeded by Hazrat Sheikh Najmeddin Tamat-al Kobra Khivaghi, the greatest sage and Sufi of his time. He trained seventeen noble disciples. Among them were Sheikh Farideddin Attar, Seyfeddin Bakharzi, and Ali Lala Ghaznavi – who succeeded him. Molana Jalaleddin Balkhi Rumi was a student of one of Hazrat Kobra's disciples. He was martyred by Mongols in 618/1221, when he was seventy eight years old.

Hazrat Ali Lala Ghaznavi was succeeded by Hazrat Sheikh Ahmad Zaker Jowzeghani who founded the *zekr* (chants of remembrance) of *la-ilaha-illa'llah* (there is no other but God). He passed away in 669/1270 in the era of Ebgha Khan, son of Holaaku Khan, and his tomb is in Kurian- Esfarayen, Iran.

He was succeeded by his son, Hazrat Noureddin Abdolrahman Esfarayeni, whom he trained from an early age to reach the highest level of cognition in Sufism. He wrote prolifically and endeavored greatly to introduce Sufism to the people of his time. He passed away in 717/1317 in Baghdad. He had trained Hazrat Sheikh Alaoddowleh Semnani to be his successor. Hazrat Semnani, who was born to a wealthy and noble family in Semnan, Iran, studied the sciences of his time, and entered the royal court at an early age. While serving in the war of Arghon-Khan, he felt a revolution in himself and began his search for cognition through worship and self-discipline. After meeting his master, Hazrat Noureddin Esfarayeni, he attained the highest state of cognition and then propagated the teachings and wrote numerous works. He passed away in 736/1335 in Borj-Ahrar Sufi Abad, Iran.

He trained Hazrat Mahmoud Mazdeghani, who was considered the greatest Sufi of the 8th/15th century, to be his successor. Hazrat Amir Seyyed Ali Hamedani, known as the second Ali, was renowned for his knowledge of the sciences and Sufism. He wrote many works and succeeded his master, Hazrat Mazdeghani.

Hazrat Sheikh Ahmad Khatlani attained the highest state of cognition through his master, Hazrat Seyyed Ali Hamedani. At the age of ninety six, by the order of Mirza Shahrokh, he was martyred in Balkh for being a Shi'a.

Hazrat Seyyed Mohammad Abdollah Ghatifi al Hasavi Nourbakhsh was an eminent personality and the Sufi of his time. Born in Gha'en in the district of Ghohestan, he was granted the title of Nourbakhsh (one who bestows light) by his master, Hazrat Khatlani. His books and treatises are detailed in *Research,*

Biography, and Works of Mohammad Nourbakhsh. He passed away in 869/1464, and his tomb is located in Souleghan, Iran. He trained Hazrat Shah Ghassem Feyzbakhsh to be his successor. Hazrat Feyzbakhsh, who was praised and highly respected by Shah Ismail Safavi, king of Iran, passed away in 927/1520. The next four masters, in succession, were Hazrat Hossein Abarghoui Janbakhsh, Hazrat Darvish Malek Ali Joveyni, Hazrat Darvish Ali Sodeyri, and Hazrat Darvish Kamaleddin Sodeyri, who was succeeded by Hazrat Darvish Mohammad Mozaheb Karandehi (known as Pir Palandouz). This great master was born in the 10th/17th century, and passed away in 1037/1627. His tomb is located in Mashad, Iran.

The next masters, again in succession, were Hazrat Mir Mohammad Mo'em Sodeyri Sabzevari, Hazrat Mir Mohammad Taghi Shahi Mashhadi, Hazrat Mir Mozafar Ali, Hazrat Mir Mohammad Ali, Hazrat Seyyed Shamseddin Mohammad, and Hazrat Seyyed Abdolvahab Naini, who was a renowned master from Yazd, Iran. He passed away at the age of ninety six, in the year 1212/1797, and his tomb is located in Nain, Iran.

Hazrat Haj Mohammad Hassan Kouzekanani was his successor.

Born in Kouzekanan, Tabriz, in 1156/1743, he passed away in Nain

in 1250/1834. In *Nassekh al-Tavarikh* is recorded the famous story of

how he met with Mohammad Shah Ghajar when Mohammad was

a young prince. He gave Mohammad a sword, saying that he would

become king of Iran. Several years later when Mohammad became

the king, he realized it was only because Hazrat Kouzekanani

had given him the sword. He was followed by Hazrat Agha

Abdolghader Jahromi.

After Sheikh Jahromi, an important event in the history of the

School took place. Hazrat Jalaleddin Ali Mir Abolfazl Angha, in

addition to receiving the leadership in the Oveyssi order from

Hazrat Jahromi, was given authority of succession by both Hazrat

Agha Mohammad Jassebi to the Maroufi, Nematollahi order,

and by Hazrat Seyyed Hossein Dezfuli to the Zahabieh order,

becoming the Pole of his time. Born in Ghazvin in 1266/1849, he

came to Tehran in 1284/1867 and attained the absolute state of

cognition through hard work, obedience, and discipline. He began

explaining Sufism in scientific terms. He passed away in Tehran

in 1339/1915.

Hazrat Mir Ghotbeddin Mohammad Angha succeeded his

father and attained a supreme position in science and Sufism. It is written of Hazrat Mir Ghotbeddin that, "If it were not for our Lord Mohammad, son of Mir Abolfazl Angha, the reality of Sufism would never have appeared in our era." Born in Tehran on May 10, 1887, he passed away on September 22, 1962, and is buried next to his father in Ebne Babvieh located in Ray, Iran.

My father, Hazrat Shah Maghsoud Sadegh Angha, succeeded his father as the forty first great master of the School. Because of his immense knowledge in so many fields and because he made Sufism accessible to the contemporary person through his voluminous writings in the sciences, philosophy, poetry, alchemy, etc, the school is now known as Maktab Tarighat Oveyssi Shahmaghsoudi. His teaching marked the advent of a new era in the history of Sufism. The truth of Islam was to be made world known. The knowledge embedded in the teachings of the *Holy Qur'an*, and the traditions of the Holy Prophet were to be announced to humanity. On September 4, 1970 my father officially appointed me as his successor, and gave me the responsibility to propagate this message to the human community.

It may seem to you that what I have said so far is history. However, if you look closely, you will discover that I have presented the fundamental points upon which Sufism rests. You will note that confirmation and appointment of each master by his predecessor is an absolute necessity. Let us take the example of Hazrat Oveys. Although he never met the Holy Prophet on the physical plane, he was nonetheless confirmed by the Holy Prophet. Hazrat Salman Farsi was directly trained and confirmed by the Holy Prophet. Each of these great masters represents a different aspect of the teachings of this School. First, the necessity of the presence of the master, and second, the inward attainment of cognition. The other important point which must not be forgotten is that this chain of transmission has never been broken from the time of the Holy Prophet to the present time, which means the light and knowledge of Islam has never been left unguarded. Just as the sun never ceases to shine, this knowledge too has been passed from master to master, so those who seek to attain their divine state will be guided toward such a goal.

Knowledge of the truth of the human being and existence has a course which goes beyond the basic preliminary messages and discoveries, and ends with absolute cognition. This innate drive and curiosity has determined the human being's destiny and fate and has completed the pages of the book of self-knowledge with the humming love-call of its seekers throughout the centuries. In each age, according to the will of Existence, a new branch appears on the tree of Life – the pre-emptor – to guide and save the sons of man.

Existence created the beautiful in manifestations, and beauty has been veiled in meanings. As it is stated in the *Holy Qur'an*, (2:257): "God is the protector of those who have faith: from the depths of darkness He will lead them forth unto light."

Now, I would like to speak on the experiential aspect of this transmitted knowledge of Sufism and its relevance to each person and to the human society – a reality for each one of you. I have defined Sufism as the reality of religion, the true human right of each person in his or her own time and the way to the realization of human perfection. If we separate human prejudices and cultural factors from the essence of the Prophets' messages, we will see that the message of each is intended to direct human beings to experience a higher state of their being. However, the only thing that remains from the teachings of the Prophets is a set of empty rituals, superstition and dogma that no intelligent human being is willing to accept. The noble and dignified rank of religion has been lost in the cobweb of the ignorance of those who claim to represent the Holy Prophets. The decadence and outdated systems of existing spiritual institutions have fostered alienation and disinterest in people. Religion has become a means of mobilizing masses of ignorant and underprivileged people by promising, them heaven or threatening them with hell. Religion in societies is no more than social gatherings or political platforms, instead of being the institutions where people are introduced to their true human dignity and are taught to be the true peacemakers of their societies.

Interfaith gatherings have become quite popular. Groups gather to discuss how they must understand each other in order to prevent religious conflicts and wars. But, they do not ask themselves, why is it that in a family, or society or country where one religion prevails, there are still so many conflicts, hatreds, and killings? These groups fail to realize that the most fundamental purpose of religion is to transform human beings from their base level to their divine level of existence. If religion truly existed in the lives of people, then greed, struggle for power and fame, envy, jealousy, etc, which are the sources for the many conflicts in the world, would cease to exist.

How many times have we seen the boundaries of nations drawn and redrawn? How many wars have erupted between societies and devastated and destroyed the lives of people? And how many civilizations have become mere ruins because of invasions?

John Foster Dulles, among others, has said that there has been a war every three years out of four in the history of man. The number of organizations promoting peace has increased dramatically, and yet the number of tribal, regional, and religious conflicts have not decreased. It is estimated that the number of violent deaths in the 20th century is close to 100 million.

What types of societies are we speaking about when we read in the headlines: "Youth kills Youth," "Getting Ready to Die Young: Surrounded by Violence, Some D.C. Youths Plan Their Own Funerals," "Youth Gets Two Life Terms in Baby Killing," "Specialists See a Youthful Version of Battered Spouse Syndrome." In the U.S.A., for example, the polls show that the first concern of the American people is crime! The spirit of despair is becoming pervasive in societies. Youth have lost their hope and respect for institutions, leaders, parents, and teachers, because they see the confusion, the corruption, and the inconsistencies that engulf their societies. Why is humanity so helpless in achieving a conclusive peace and harmonious and tranquil societies? What will it take for humans to realize that they must look at peace from a different perspective?

The basic unit of any society is the human being. If this unit is not known, how then can effective laws, programs, structures, educational, and economic systems be devised to meet its needs? As I mentioned earlier, the correct word for Sufism is *Irfan*, derived from the word *ma'rifa*, which means to know, to cognize. When can we say we know something? When nothing about the subject of study remains unknown to us.

Is it not amazing that with such extensive researches being conducted in the biological, behavioral, social, and psychological sciences, no conclusive results in knowing this complex organism have yet been attained? The intricate mechanism and functions of this organism, which has an average volume of somewhat more than a cubic yard and an average weight of 170 pounds, are so complex that one expert is unable to diagnose all its aspects independently. Distinct specialized and sub-specialized branches had to be developed to give a more complete assessment of each aspect.

Over 1,400 years ago the Prophet of Islam said, "Whoever cognizes their true self has cognized God." The true self is not the changing cellular system, the social conditionings, nor the mental and emotional states that are constantly in a state of flux and change. The true self is the stable reality, the true personality of each human being. In Islam it is equated with the Divine. This is why Islam proclaims the Oneness of Existence – "la-ilaha-illa'llah –there is no other but God." This is the true human dignity granted to humans, that there is no separation between you and God. As it is stated in the *Holy Qur'an* (50:16), "I am closer to you than your jugular vein."

Religion is a discipline, a precise system of training, whereby each person is individually trained to discover a dimension within his or her own being where the divine attributes are manifested. It is the realization of attributes such as compassion, knowledge, selflessness, love, devotion, honor, trust, etc – the attributes that are normally associated with saints of the past. This is the dimension of their being that the Prophets discovered through their cognition of God that gave rise to their uniqueness, strength, and knowledge.

When people are trained to discover the inner dimension of their being, then willingly they will leave behind their savage attributes which give rise to greed, injustice, hatred and violence. What is the result of such a discovery? If each individual is trained to stand on his or her own strength, would such persons be needy? Will they not see their own uniqueness and the strength that this uniqueness brings? If each person is trained to develop his or her own talents and abilities, will there be any room for insecurity, jealousy, or envy? Will they be lacking anything? Will they need to compete with anyone?

In 1973, sixteen scientific questions were addressed to my father by the International Multidisciplinary Research Association.[8] The questions posed by these scientists centered around major problems of modern science which are of critical importance to the improvement of the mental and physical well-being of humanity, to ecological harmony, and even to the actual continuation of human life on this planet. Several questions concerned competition: "Why do organisms compete with one another instead of cooperating (or loving, as in the case of humans)?" Why do trees compete and kill one another for a place in the sun? Why don't they form one great organism, and why do individual parts of organisms accept the influence of other parts, but collectively continue to struggle? The question was quite lengthy and ultimately leads to inter-cellular communication and healing, a topic which would require a lengthy discussion and cannot be discussed at this time.

I think my father's response to these scientists will clarify many points for you. He states that if we put the question differently, we might see that all organisms and parts of organisms, are cooperating in life. A particle loses nothing when it is eaten by another. The billions of plants which we conceive of as living separately, are each in fact an agent of life that influence and are influenced and changed by interactions with all other life forms. Each particle continues until unfavorable conditions occur, at which point it is dissolved (we call this death) and then transformed into another form, thus continuing its life a new. Life continues, regardless of the form it may take.

"Perhaps it would be better to say that cellular life lacks

competition." In the infinite unity of existence, there are no conflicts and no antagonisms. Humanity, in attempting to explain reality, has sometimes thought that the transient world remains preserved somehow, in some non-material spiritual form. However the units of measurement accepted by science conceal the spiritual, non-material realm, making it impossible for us to perceive or even conceptualize such a world. For example, water presents contrasting forms depending on its state. We know of liquid, ice, or steam, but the true structure of water is concealed. The same is true of all other matter. "Although matter has different manifestations, its genuine reality is never lost, and nothing is either increased or decreased."

What cell or molecule can feed or struggle beyond its capability? Not a single one; otherwise it would upset the equilibrium of its life. We see ourselves and all other matter as individuals, separated and isolated from each other, for our senses prevent us from knowing the essence of our being and the true unity of all existence. In a young tree, we see separate branches and leaves, yet it is nourished through its life span by a root provided by existence, through the unity of being which makes a tree a tree. In appearances we behold the separateness of nature, but the infinite existence is the only nurturer, just as it is with the branches and leaves. Everything is interdependent and sustained by the unifying force of existence.

"The world of creation is a painted surface. If everything in the painting was only one color and monotonous, it would not cheer anyone. It is the variety of contrasting colors which cause human beings, animals, plants, and inanimate objects to be worthy of note."

The business community is finally shifting its focus from competition to cooperation. It has now seen that when cooperation exists, productivity and job satisfaction are increased. As a result there are less job turnovers, less absenteeism, less job-related stress and stress-induced illnesses. Since cooperation translates into more profit for the company, the business community therefore promotes it.

In a society where children are taught that they must compete in order to get ahead, how can they not be expected to step over others in order to become successful? Are not social structures founded upon race, color, religion, ethnicity, etc.? Aren't these the elements used to foster hatred and separation? Isn't it time to see that what appears as diversity is a reflection of an underlying unity, and diversity can be a source for creativity and not conflict? If people are able to see that race, gender, and ethnicity have no bearing on human dignity, will so much hatred and animosity exist? After all, does the soul have a gender, race, color or creed?

Hopelessness, insecurities, and strife exist in societies because people have not found the stable source of their existence. During the historical span of time which appears to be so long, the universe has continued with tranquility and peace throughout its orbital revolutions without ever faltering. What law prevails in this nearly infinite journey that governs all entities and their precise interrelationships, and prevents any disorder in their development and evolutionary motion as presented in the manifestation of nature?

Recognition and discovery of this specific principle, the source which causes a relative permanence for such matter and celestial bodies that may appear without "intelligence", may be invaluable in reaching a deeper and more conclusive understanding of peace. Because in Sufism, recognition of the true sense of religion, the ultimate goal of the Holy Prophets and Saints, has been the attainment of an ideal state which is synonymous with eternity

and final peace. It is stated in the *Holy Qur'an* (40:64):

> "He – God who placed the earth as your foundation and
> the sky as the axis of your organizer constructed your
> figure to perfection, and gave you blessed sustenance;
> This is Allah, your Protector, who is Great – the Protector
> of mankind."

If we observe the structures of the smallest particle to the largest

celestial bodies, we will see that the existence of each entity is

founded upon a structure, and yet these structures are hidden to

the naked eye. Cognition of God within the heavenly realm of each

individual is like a seed that a gardener plants in a fertile ground

and looks after, day in and day out, until that seed undergoes its

complete cycle of growth and bears its fruit.

If you look at the growth process of a seed, you will see that

the necessary structure for its evolutionary process to move from

seed to fruit was foreseen in the seed itself. The place where the

seed grows, and the conditions under which it grows, determine

how many of the existing structures are activated into realization.

The healthy growth of the root determines the future of the stem,

branches, leaves, flowers and fruits. Each stage of the growth is

dependent upon the completion and health of the preceding stage.

To manifest its ultimate stage of completion, each stage of growth must be in a state of health, and in harmony with the pre- vailing environmental conditions.

The human being has a highly developed and intricate structure. Overall, the human being relates and interacts through the following four different levels that comprises his axis of search, thought and being:

First, the mysterious inner level, which is the central point of stability of the human being's character and identity;

Second, the developmental level, which is the locus for the development and interrelationship of the magnetic bodies as well as the mental, sensory, and psychic powers;

Third, the dependent, indigent and impressed cellular level, which in fact is the mechanical level of the human being;

Fourth, nature, which is the locus for the material manifestations and exchanges - the laboratory for the examination and experimentation of man's aptitudes, and the place to satisfy his needs. Each level has different requirements for its existence, and yet it is dependent on the previous level for its health and balance. While the physical level needs nature for its sustenance, it is dependent on the health and stability of the electromagnetic system, which in turn is sustained through its connection with the source of life in the heart. My father, Hazrat Shah Maghsoud Sadegh Angha has explained this in detail in his book, *The Hidden Angles of Life.*

If you look closely, you will see that the fragrance of the flower has no resemblance to its roots in the soil, and yet the roots are necessary for the growth of the flower and the presence of the fragrance. The entire growth process was intended for that fragrance to emerge. The fragrance would not have evolved, had the flower not completed its full cycle of growth under stable conditions. Whereas the flower is grounded to the roots through the stem, the fragrance is unbounded and free. For reflective people, nature can be an eloquent teacher showing the laws of Existence.

The prescribed rites of religion are a means for humans to re-establish their connection with their inner level, from which they are estranged. It is stability in this level that frees the soul from being under the domination of the earthly appetites of the human being. The instructions given by the Holy Prophets provide the necessary structure to free the soul from enslavement, so that humans may attain their true rank as is created in the image of God. The soul is the divine essence present within each human being. Where reliance resides in God, can despair ever be present? What is the fruit of reliance on God, but hope, prosperity, tranquility and peace?

My father, in his book *Nirvan*, has said that "On the seventh day, man was housed in the Empyrean. A sound of hope echoed in the infinite existence: 'Nonentity is not, and unique Existence is.' Nirvan, who had left the world of appearances, thrust away the dust, lost his identity in the infinite, and regained peace."[9]

How do we measure whether or not what we have done has been effective? By the results we obtain. What is the measurement for knowing we have "religion"? The result of having religion should show in the presence of peace, stability and hope in our lives. Despair and hope cannot reside side by side; nor, can hatred and love; or greed and compassion. Tell me, if you have God, what else do you need? Doesn't 100 include 1 through 99?

My father, in his book *Dawn*, has said, "The wise are those who acquire benefits and repel losses."[10] It is up to each person to decide what he or she wishes to cultivate and grow. Existence is infinite, and infinite possibilities are available at each instant for each person. What course do you want to choose on this infinite journey of no return?

May God plant the seed of prosperity, hope and peace in the land of your heart.

ENDNOTES

1. Quoted in the preface to al-Muqaddisi, Sheikh Izzidin. (1980). *Revelation of the Secrets of the Birds and Flowers*. London: Octagon Press.

2. See Schimmel, Annemarie. (1975). Mystical *Dimensions of Islam*.Chapel Hill: University of North Carolina Press.

3. See Nicholson, Reynold A. (1989). *The Mystics of Islam*. London: Arkana.

4. See Izutsu, Toshihiko, (1994). *Creation and the Timeless Order of Things*. Ashland, OR: White Cloud Press.

5. See, for example, Smith Margaret. (1978). *The Way of the Mystics*. NY: Oxford University Press.

6. Hujwiri, Ali B. Uthman al-Jullabi. (1978). *Kashf al-Mahjub of al-Hujwiri*. London: E.J.W. Gibb Memorial.

7. *Mystical Dimensions of Islam*, p. 28.

8. The responses to these questions were published in *The Hidden Angles of Life*, by Molana al-Moazam Hazrat Shah Maghsoud Sadegh Angha. (1975). Pomona, CA: Multidisciplinary Publications.

9. Angha, Molana al-Moazam Hazrat Shah Maghsoud Sadegh. (1986). *The Mystery of Humanity: Survival and Tranquility*. Lanham: University Press of America. p. 36.

10. Angha, Molana al-Moazam Hazrat Shah Maghsoud Sadegh. (1989). *Dawn*. Lanham: University Press of America. p. 31.

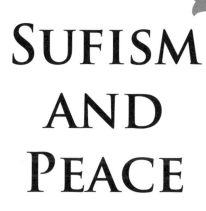

SUFISM
AND
PEACE

In the Name of God
Most Gracious, Most Merciful

"There is another way of action and belief – one not bound to custom, tradition, race, culture, personal or social ideologies — yet capable of changing the course of human destiny."

Peace and Human Rights – these are words which create strong emotional feelings in everyone. But what do they really mean? How much of the meaning is known to those who use these words so frequently? And how much of the meaning is known to those who listen to the promises of Peace and Human Rights?

When communication is based on "unknowns", the "known" cannot be obtained, and positive and effective results cannot be realized. How can you give someone something you yourself do not have? How can you give when you don't know what it is that you are giving? Is it possible to define something when you don't know what it is?

Wasn't it only a few years ago that Yasser Arafat was considered a terrorist? What has changed within these few short years? Who had called him a terrorist, and who calls him a peace-maker now? Who sets these criteria? What is the measure with which the criteria are set? Aren't these questions that should be raised in the mind of any thoughtful and rational human being before making decisions?

Dreaming of peace is not Peace!

Everyone speaks of peace and yet there is no peace.

Everyone wants peace and yet we have no peace. Each human being's innate urge is to live in peace, and yet people do not cease fighting, killing and destroying.

We do not have true peace or real human rights today. Have we ever had them in the history of humanity? It is said that peace prevailed at the time of the *Pax Romana*. What we have had since the beginning of recorded time is ever constant disputes, confrontations, conflicts and wars. Humanity's state has been one of constant agitation, uncertainty, hardship and tribulation, combined with the erosion of basic human values in society.

The actions of peace groups whether international or not, result not in the implementation of peace, but rather in the temporary elimination of disputes which, in effect, protects and perpetuates the gains of existing powers. The essential goal of peace has always seemed beyond reach. Even where there is no outright warfare, we find continuing policies of political and economic exploitation, and the prevalence of inequalities.

Economic exploitation takes different forms, and the appearance of "human rights" is proudly advertised by many nations. The ruthless economic competition, the financial manipulations of multinational companies; the sometimes precarious state of worldwide economies and the monetary system; the periodic booms and busts of the world's stock markets; the billions of dollars of debt of numerous nations, both developed and developing; and the shaky economic state of the world's banking system, are all means of exploitation of the weak by the strong.

Peacekeepers, peacemakers, peace organizations, and peace institutes continue to grow in numbers, and yet we do not have peace.

A true understanding of the words "human rights", "personality", and "identity" is crucial in planning for as well as moving toward peaceful societies. These words are defined according to the cultural, political, and social perspectives of each society. For example, promoting women's rights may be a major political and social concern in one country, in another it may seem irrelevant, and in still another it may go against the grain of the social fabric of that society. If child labor is an acceptable means of survival for one family in one country, in another country it is considered unacceptable and is made illegal. The endless debates we saw over the abortion issue at the recent population conference in Cairo is another example of this dilemma.

Let us take the words "human rights". What is commonly known as "human rights" is a person's right to vote, to free speech, to free press and etc. And, it is generally agreed among "democratic" governments that if these rights are not provided, then people's human rights are violated. If you ask the same people to define what they mean by a human being, they will most probably give you a definition that sums up the human being as the sum total of his or her needs, actions and reactions.

All disciplines – from physical, political, economic, social, psychological, and philosophical viewpoints – have attempted to define the human being. If you look closely at any of the descriptions provided by the above groups, you will see that their definitions are based on their observations of the interaction of the electro-chemical processes of the physical level with the external environment.

Let me take a moment and give a few examples. Scientists run experiments, dissect organs, and perform sophisticated operations, not only to provide effective treatments for problems, but also to present a comprehensive view of the human being. The intricate mechanisms and functions of the human being, which has an average volume of somewhat more than a cubic yard and weighs an average of 170 pounds, are so complex that they exceed the capacity of even the most brilliant and intelligent scientists to totally understand. Numerous specialties and sub-specialties in the field of medicine have evolved to diagnose and provide complete and thorough assessment of various illnesses.

Psychologists and psychoanalysts have also presented advanced theories based upon their observation of the human being's actions and reactions within society. What psychology originally intended to study was the "psyche" – the word for "soul" in Greek. However, what it actually does study is the behavior of the human being in its various forms of relationships, whereas the study of the "soul", as was originally intended, has escaped their attention.

Researchers in the fields of economics, political science and the social sciences, in general, define the human being as a social unit with needs and dependencies, fulfilling the roles of both producer and consumer in a materialistic society. Theoretical philosophers and social ideologues envision a self-sufficient and prosperous society. They look for Utopia and construct grand schemes to realize the "ideal society" where order is based upon total obedience to a social system.

If we take any of the above definitions of the human being, and put them next to any of the human rights categories mentioned earlier, we will see that what is spoken of are actually "people's rights" and not "human rights". You are probably wondering what I mean by this. Let me explain it in this manner:

The most fundamental principle of Sufism is, "unless a subject is completely known, its benefits and, ultimately, the necessity to make effective plans for its implementation, can never be realized". This principle is applied to knowing the human being, peace, and the human rights — and knowing one of these completely is to know them all.

Lets us take a comprehensive look at the human being. The cause and motive for all movements toward war and peace, the ultimate judge of all things, the repository of all societal strengths, as well as weaknesses – is that moving, complex creature called the "human being". The human being is endowed with physical and mental powers, with mind, reasoning, emotions, imagination, and will. Furthermore, the human being is the result of millions of years of evolutionary development.

The human being's different dimensions, which are among the wonders of existence, have extensive relationships with both their internal and external environments. The human being in its limited physical state, confined within the dimensions of space, time and place, is also endowed with other attributes which have not received sufficient attention. The resulting human being is not only a synthesis of all these functions, but is also a repository of embedded knowledge.

Just as precious diamonds do not dissolve into the sludge of swamps, and the running veins of pure gold keep their luminosity within the heart of the earth and are loath to mix with the brittle soil in mines, so does the human being bear a distinctive attribute in its 'earthly natural being, which is also luminous and has a separate life to undertake. The human being is of earth, but is not mortal. And in the midst of the darkness of nature, the human essence remains unswerving and constant.

This is the dimension that distinguishes the human being from other creatures. In the teachings of Islam, the true identity of the human being is equated with the Divine, as proclaimed by the words, *"la-illaha-illa'llah"* – "there is no other but God". As the Holy Prophet Mohammad (peace and blessings upon him) has said, "Whoever cognizes their true self, has cognized God." The true rank of the human being exceeds any definition that is provided by the various disciplines mentioned earlier.

In other words, the true human right of each individual is the realization of his or her rank as created in the image of God. To understand this statement, we must know and understand the most vital urges of the human being, and know how these urges are translated and expressed through its multi–operative levels.

Let us take this example first. One of the most fundamental needs of the human being is survival. Some may call it self-preservation. Why is there such a need, where does it come from, and how can it be properly understood? On the natural physical level, this urge is translated to mean that the human being will do everything in its power to live, much like other living entities in the world. Therefore, it seeks food, shelter and etc in order to survive. Reproduction is generally seen as an extension of the need to survive. Therefore, all human activities are geared, first, towards the protection of this level of existence – feeding, clothing, and protecting the physical body.

However, we see that even when these needs are met, people are not satisfied. The urge to survive takes on a new dimension. If today, bread and water are seen as enough for survival, tomorrow they will be replaced by bread and cheese, the next day by steak and wine, and so on. If today, a roof over the head is sufficient, tomorrow it will be a house, the next day a mansion, and so on. Those who have more, want more. Those who do not are pushed further and further into a mere survival mode.

Aggression, greed, oppression, etc. are linked to the human being's identification with earthly life. Fame, wealth, credibility, worldliness, scholarship, and power, are methods through which people are classified and ranked. Therefore, people's identity becomes dependent upon the various social, political, economic, and educational systems whose standards have already been pre-determined by their societies and cultures. Moreover, people begin to adopt and adapt these pre-determined measures as standards after which they model their personalities. Since identities and personalities become associated with worldly accomplishments, people strive to accumulate more wealth, more power, more fame, and so on. In order to maintain their power, the aggressors continue to oppress, and the oppressed grow in numbers.

Meanwhile, each human being wants to live in peace. The more people engage in worldly pursuits, the more disquiet they become. The affluent and the needy both search for peace. The oppressor and the oppressed both search for methods to numb their disquiet, through lavish lifestyles, alcohol, drugs, violence, or the hope of revenge, while masses of the ignorant are easily led astray by placing all their worries in a blind faith that promises a peaceful and permanent repose in heaven as a reward for their good deeds. In summary, since the human being sees its survival and identity to be dependent on the physical world, whether physically, emotionally or socially, its appetite for the world becomes insatiable. You can apply this principle to all levels of interaction in society. You can apply it to the smallest unit, the family, or to the largest, the world community. You see relationships, partnerships, friendships, marriages, come together and fall apart, because the personalities and identities people fabricate for themselves are based upon the standards set by their societies, all arising from the unknown roots of the urge to survive.

If you pay close attention to the physiological system of the human being, you will see that in order to survive, each cell absorbs, assimilates and repels. This is the law governing all living organisms. If the cell does not repel, but simply gathers and accumulates, imbalance will occur and it will not survive.

As long as human beings interact only from their earthly level of human attachments and needs, then greed, injustice, enmity, and inequality will continue to prevail. The instructions of all the Prophets, and especially those of the Prophet Mohammad (peace and blessings upon him) are intended to guide human beings to know their reality, so they may live in balance, peace, and know their eternity. If human beings discover their eternity, their urge for survival will be fulfilled. The fear of death will no longer press them toward seeking earthly fulfillments, which ultimately leads to imbalance and destruction. Nor will they accept false identities and personalities. They will know that their reality is not bounded by the pre-fabricated structures dictated by society.

Therefore, what is commonly referred to as "human rights" should be corrected to say "people's rights". Yes, society, government, organizations, institutions, etc. can make provisions to improve the standards of living of people. But human rights cannot be forced upon people. Human rights can only be attained through education. If each person were trained to know his or her reality – the true human personality and dignity – could anyone add or take anything away from them? Could dictatorships exist? Could aggression and exploitation exist? Will the result of such a system of training not bring about peace and democracy?

Democracy cannot be forced upon people. It must arise from the people and be sustained by the people, so that it may grow and become strong. It was only last month that the U.S. decided to invade Haiti to re-establish democracy. Anything which is forced upon people will not endure, for the foundation and structure will not be there to provide the necessary support.

The simplest and the most general definition for society is that of a system consisting of its people and their behaviors. If we look at any level of contemporary society, we will see that peace does not exist. We see love turn to hatred, partnerships turn to feuds, and families dismantled.

Furthermore, if we look at the statistics of suicide, murder, rape, child abuse, domestic violence, and incest, we cannot help but to stop and note that there must be something wrong. People turn to food, drugs, and alcohol to numb their restlessness and anxieties. Addiction has reached children in the primary grades, and yet educators refuse to look at the situation from a different perspective.

The educational systems should be revised, so children can be effectively educated to know their true human rights, their true personality and true identity. The system of education should provide a conducive environment where the talents and abilities of children are developed, so children can realize their true self-worth and stand on their own strength. If children are trained from this perspective, they will not be drawn into the many addictive and destructive patterns of behavior that dominate the lives of the adults, and plague societies around the world.

I believe it is time that world leaders, educators, and researchers take a good look at the result of their past efforts; put aside partisanship, prejudice, and narrow-mindedness, and change the existing educational system. Unless these changes are made and the future generations are trained to know their true human rights, there will be no hope for peace, democracy and survival.

We must not think that we need to undertake monumental and intricate projects to attain this goal. It is my opinion that instead of persisting on trying to design and implement an illusory idea known as society, thinkers and leaders should put their efforts towards providing the means by which individuals can be guided to know their true values. The resulting society will then enjoy prosperity, happiness and equality. If each human being is trained to develop all of his/her inherent talents and abilities, then they will be able to stand against baseless and unfounded ideas at any cost. They shall know the true meaning of "prosperity for human society," and will have sound, constructive ideas and actions.

Sufism is the method of instruction of all the Holy Prophets, and the way to introduce each person individually to his or her inherent values and true personality. Sufism, in its teachings, is the educational method through which the human being is reconciled with the heavenly kingdom. The human being is, therefore, trained to develop all of its creative abilities so that he or she may benefit from all the resources provided by nature, and live in peace, knowledge and justice.

Unless organizations which serve as innovators for social and educational changes discover a constant spiritual measure, disparate and changeable factors such as prejudice and differences in attitudes will not be eliminated. The more we strive toward this goal with all existing resources – natural, material, and above all, human – the sooner we shall reach tangible results and the sooner will the foundation for a unified and a stable social system, based upon true human values and relationships, be implemented.

To summarize, the happiness and prosperity to which humanity has envisioned and aspired, will prevail only when all individuals benefit from a state of spiritual well-being. A successful human society is attained through the outward and inward harmony of each of its members, and their harmonious existence within a unified system. Without achieving this, all international laws and agreements, and all organizations which use the term "peace" as a concept without its true realization, will fail in creating a prosperous and peaceful society with the existing methods.

To arrive at a comprehensive understanding of the human being it is required that we distinguish between "real peace" and "pre-fabricated peace", between "human rights", and "people's rights", and between "life" and "living". What system can be more powerful than a society where people have recognized their true human dignity and human rights? Can anything but peace prevail in such a society?

In closing, let me quote a verse from the *Holy Qur'an* (50:6):

> "Do they not look at the sky above them?
> How we have made it; And adorned it,
> And there are no flaws in it?"

If existence can create such perfection, with balance and harmony, then surely we do not need to look very far to find the same perfection, balance and harmony.

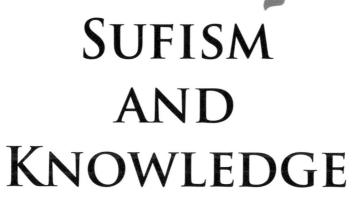

SUFISM
AND
KNOWLEDGE

In the Name of God
Most Gracious, Most Merciful

God Most Gracious!

It is He Who has taught the Qur'an.

He has created man:

He has taught him speech.

The sun and the moon follow courses computed;

And the herbs and the trees

Both bow in adoration

And the Firmament has He

Raised high, and He has set up the Balance,

In order that ye may not transgress balance.

So establish weight with justice

And fall not short in the balance.

(Holy Qur'an, 55:1-9)

P raise is for God, the All-Knowing, the All-Wise, who bestowed the cloak of knowledge upon His chosen, and conferred the Robe of Glory and Balance in its perfection upon all creation; and set in motion the earth and heavens with His exalted grace and wisdom so that they may be the abode of cognition and affection; and within the infinite core of man, He placed the measure of balance, justice and love to be the guiding light for the elevation of man's being towards the Supreme Essence of Existence.

Thank you for inviting me to speak at your university — the city of knowledge and the city of creation, which is the foundation of the universe.

When we observe the universe, we see how peaceful it is; how tranquil it is. The reason is knowledge; the reason is stability. The universe is all knowledge. If it is possible to have stability and tranquility in the vast universe, which expands from nowhere to nowhere, with no beginning and no end, then we should see the same tranquility and stability in the smaller units – from the atom to human societies – since they are a part of the universe.

Can we agree that where knowledge and wisdom exist, ignorance, abuse and hatred cannot exist? It is in this context that I would like to speak about Sufism.

Sufism is the reality of religion. In essence, it is a method, a way, a discipline that teaches each person the science of exploring his or her being, unearthing his or her hidden talents and potentials, and discovering the reality of his or her being in this unbounded and infinite tapestry called existence. This process is not a result of the functioning of the mental faculties, i.e., induction, deduction, analysis, etc. It is the method and the way through which the Prophets attained the state of absolute cognition.

In the teachings of Sufism, the human being is considered as the perfect image of the universe – the macrocosm and the microcosm – from the physical, magnetic, and metaphysical, to the very depths of the black hole; that is, if we can use this image of existence. Whatever exists in this universe also exists in the human being. Over 1,400 years ago, Amir al-Mo'menin Ali (peace be upon him) said:

"Do you ponder that you are microcosm?
Contained within you is the macrocosm,
And you are the Clear Book whose words
Manifest the inner."

If we look objectively and closely at the human being, we cannot

but be amazed and in awe of this exquisite and unique masterpiece

of creation, operated by the will of knowledge whose silent hand

has unwrapped the potential of beings into manifestations, so

that the pages of existence may be adorned with the beauty of its

wisdom.

The physiological or mechanical dimension of the human being

not only undergoes the total evolutionary process during its life

cycle as a fetus – from the mineral form of its elements, to its

plant-like blossoming growth, to the animal form of recapitulated

development, to its final human form – but also contains all the

elements present in the realm of nature. This is the level of the

human being that interacts with nature, is nurtured by nature, and

ultimately returns to nature.

If we look at the various medical and scientific fields, it is easy

to see how complex the human being is. How many branches of

science exist because they want to understand how the human

system functions? How many disciplines exist that examine and study the mental and emotional aspects of the human being? How many "religions" or "sects" claim to know how to redeem the human soul? Have any of these disciplines come to a conclusive and satisfying result or understanding of the human being?

Most, if not all of the scientific disciplines exist because they want to make the "natural" life of people more comfortable, less painful, and ultimately much longer. Have the advances in the scientific fields or psycho-social disciplines resulted in creating peaceful individuals, societies and nations? Have any of the religious, political, or social leaders managed to do so?

The evolutionary stages of life on earth, and the capacity of life forms to adapt in order to survive, are self-evident signs that knowledge has no boundaries and limitations. Where can you look in this universe that you will not see the manifestation of knowledge?

Why don't peace, tranquility, and knowledge prevail in human societies? Do you think if wisdom and knowledge prevailed in human societies, there would be hatred, wars, and unrest?

The signs and symptoms of disease, disorder and disaster are manifest in all aspects of human life – from the individual, to the family, to the community, and to the national and the international infrastructures. The globe is characterized by a pervasive fear and mistrust, as well as by greed expressed in continual struggles for acquisition of possessions and power. We live in a time of immense change, turbulence, violence and chaos.

At the individual level, people feel unloved, inadequate, lonely, and alienated. Fear, depression and anxiety are everyday experiences. Stress levels are high as people react to external pressures. The American Medical Association states that more than 80% of visits to physician's offices are for stress-related illnesses.[1] Alcohol and drug abuse is rampant, as people try to escape the pain and pressures of every-day life. Relationships have deteriorated, and families have split apart. Men and women neglect their children. Single women with children have become a new poverty class. Women and children are abused and molested[2]. And suicide is on the rise.

At the local level, the numbers of violent crimes have risen to alarming rates. In the U.S. "Between 1983 and 1993, the murder rate in young men 18 to 24 doubled. In boys 14 to 17, it more than doubled."[3]

At the global level we see the devastation of human lives through increased tensions, wars, and conflicts. In the wars since 1945, 60% of the casualties have been civilians – primarily women and children.[4] Around the world, the natural environment is being destroyed. Air and waters are increasingly polluted, crops and animals are adulterated with poisonous chemicals, and oxygen-giving trees are being cut down.

As national budgets are depleted to fights crimes, and drug uses, to build prisons, to increase the police force, and to develop sophisticated arms, and so on, people are put under further pressure to work harder and pay more taxes. It seems that there is no end to this vicious cycle.

These are all symptoms of an underlying illness that has not yet been diagnosed. With so much advancement in the sciences and psycho-social disciplines, not only do we not see improvements in human behavior patterns, but we see their deterioration. At least twenty years ago there was no need to have armed guards patrolling hallways in public schools, and children did not kill children.

Since the human being is the cause behind this unrest, the

subject of study in the various scientific, social, and psychological fields, as well as the experimenter and the executioner of all the laws in human societies, it is important to see him from a different perspective than is commonly used.

Hazrat Shah Maghsoud Sadegh Angha has said, "Man is a complete being, consisting of the earth and the heavens, the first endowed with fierce, beastly, and satanic attributes, and the second with divine attributes, that is, knowledge, cognition, and wisdom; and man encompasses the totality of all objects and thus he is called the chosen of creation."[5]

In the natural dimension consisting of sensual powers and instincts, the human being is a mass of cells, moving and reacting through the stimulation of insatiable needs, wishes and desires, and false appetites. As he endeavors to satisfy these needs and desires to their optimum, he creates an imbalance in himself and in his surroundings. He strives for power, money, prestige, and etceteras. The more he has, the more he wants, as natural appetite is insatiable. All these drives, often spurred by environmental factors, make him like a beast ruled by fierceness and savagery.

On this level of natural existence, like the other living

organisms, he follows the natural laws of absorption, assimilation, accumulation and repulsion. But because he rejects true balance, he does not control his appetites and desires, and contrary to most other creatures, he does not refrain from destroying and abusing natural resources, as well as personal and social relationships.

In these dimensions of thoughts and tendencies, the human being is a slave to his desires, with no alternative but to follow his destructive master, each desire leading to other insatiable desires with unknown ends. Is this the human being who is supposed to be the chosen one of creation and created in the image of God?

An important principle in Sufism is that although the human being is manifested in the natural world, his true identity is other than the sum of his natural appetites and behaviors.

Just like other organisms in nature, the physical dimension of the human consists mostly of water, and the remainder is minerals, chemicals, salts, etc. This isn't a "being". A piece of wood, a rock, a flower, an animal and a human are all similar in terms of the composition of the various elements in their physiology. However, it is his "being" which distinguishes the human from other life forms on earth. It is the "being" that has created the human.

It is the "being" who is the subject of the message of the Prophets. The Prophets are not addressing the elements that make up the various organs including the brain, the memory and the senses. They are not addressing the behaviors learned through the various socialization processes. They are addressing the "being" who has existed ever since the baby was born, and continues to be constant throughout the changes that the child undergoes until it reaches adulthood. Everything changes – the body, ideas, ideals, thoughts, goals, etc. – but the "being" called "I" always remains constant.

In essence, this is the message of all Prophets throughout time: Know yourself. Know the "being" who is everlasting and not restricted to the body, to desires, and all the actions and reactions that take place continuously. Know the "being" who is your true identity; the source of your becoming; the source of knowledge; so you may live in peace and balance; so you may know your eternity.

Having discovered and cognized their true identity, the Prophets (peace be upon them) announced to the people of their time how they had arrived at such a result. They did not say follow us blindly. They said, put to the test of personal experience what we say. Be like the scientist who endeavors to know to the fullest, the subject of his experiment and study.

For example, Buddha, after having seen suffering, left his life as a prince and embarked on the path of discovering the cause of suffering and how one could be released from it. He did not stop until he had discovered the answer.

Abraham's discovery was that one must shatter all idols, so that one can know and submit to the one God. It is through this cognition and submission that one can be released of all attachments and desires.

Moses said, by obeying the Ten Commandments, earthly appetites and impulses are controlled, and one can live in peace and tranquility, which will result in residing with peace and tranquility in the Promised Land.

Jesus said, you must be released from all your acquired earthly traits before you can enter the kingdom of heaven. He called upon a child and said, "Unless you become like this child, you will never enter the kingdom of heaven". (Matt. 18:2-3)

And, Mohammad gave directives as to how one can cognize one's true self. He said, "Whoever cognizes his true self has

cognized God." To attain this state, one must be submitted to God.
It is through submission that one's actions will be founded upon
knowledge and wisdom, and not on ignorance, superstition, and
blind faith. He has said, "The best amongst you is he whose actions
manifest his wisdom."

Every single duty in Islam, as ordained by God, is a step and a
method toward self-knowledge. Each and every duty has a reality
behind it which must be experienced within each person. In Islam,
any act of devotion which is void of its reality is considered as null.
Anything that comes between the believer and God is duality.

God commanded the Prophet of Islam,

> "O Ahmad, if my servant keeps his prayers as those of
> the world and heaven, and keeps his fast as those of the
> earth and heaven, and if he abstains from nourishment
> as the angels, and if he be naked of garment, and if he
> sees in his heart love for the world, hypocrisy or pride,
> I shall turn his heart until he withdraws, and I shall not
> give him the sweet taste of my affection.[6]"

If one looks at the life of the Prophets, one cannot but see a stable
security, self-control, humanity, compassion, and determination
that could not be shaken by the most formidable events. The law
that has governed the lives of the Prophets has been the law of
submission, and their wisdom and knowledge are rooted in this

law.

Unfortunately, the majority of people think that to be submitted means you are subservient to someone. No, that is blind faith, and not worthy of the dignity of the human being as ordained by God. Submission is the vitality of Islam. Because of the dynamic evolution and revolution that takes place within the core of the believer, where all boundaries of separation and duality cease to exist, and in truthfulness the believer attests to the oneness of God, by saying, *"la-ilaha-illa'llah"* – there is no other but God. Attestation is not only verbal, but the believer's body, mind, and heart – his entire being – must resonate with the presence of the one God.

God Almighty has said:

> "My servant endlessly seeks closeness to Me through sacrifice so that I may love him; so when I love him, I shall be the eyes with which he sees, and the ears with which he hears, the tongue with which he speaks, the hands with which he holds, the steps with which he endeavors; thus he shall see by Me, and he shall hear by Me, and he shall speak by Me, and he shall hold by Me.[7] "

This is the law of submission, where the self bounded to earthly attachments ceases to be, and only God exists. The message and instructions of Islam are meant to bring about this revolution in the person who wants to know who he or she really is. The School of the Prophets is the School of Self-Knowledge.

If we look at the human body we see harmony and balance. In the human body each organ functions independently, and yet works in harmony with the rest of the system for one purpose: the good of the whole which ensures the survival of the part. This law governs all entities in the universe. We see the fingers are submitted to the hand, the hand to the brain, and so on. They work as one unit. From the molecules, to the cells, to the organs, they work as a community and in harmony with each other, even though they live the cellular law which governs each individually. The reason for this vast cooperation is that each entity (from the small to the large) is submitted to its own inherent knowledge. Knowledge and entity are one and the same.

For any system to be formed, first there must be attraction among the composing elements. *It is the attractive field which is transformed into either energy or matter.* For example, although Albert Einstein discovered his famous equation E=mc2, he did not conclude that matter is energy or vice versa. He only spoke about the two being equivalent (i.e., of equal value). Ever since Einstein's discovery, scientists have endeavored to find the ultimate nature of matter, but as of yet they have not been successful. The conversion of matter to energy and energy to matter is always through attraction. In the fusion of two hydrogen atoms, for example, energy is emitted and the total mass is reduced. From the foregoing explanation, we can conclude that the attractive field converts to the released energy.

For the formation to actually take place, the attracting elements must converge into a state of harmony. For that system to function at its optimum, all elements composing that system must be in harmony. In the definition of a single cell, it has been said that when the physical, chemical, gravitational and universal forces act in harmony, the cell appears (or is formed). This cell contains all the physical aspects of the universe and also contains all the forces, power, or energy which have enabled it to act and react in its current state. I have called this "The Principle of Harmony".

It is mathematically shown that the energy distribution of the proton in space determines how much energy should be invested by the electron. In other words, the electron follows the field of the proton to determine the energy distribution of the hydrogen atom. The part with the smaller total energy submits to the part with greater total energy. This is "The Principle of Submission."

Finally, the electron invests as much energy as it is allowed to invest. The result of matching these two positive and negative fields is light. The energy distribution of the shared light is twice as much as that which each particle would have in space. Half of this shared light leaves this "united" system of the "H" atom. I have called this, "The Principle of Unity". That is, the result of harmony and submission of one system to another is "Unity."

Thus, the "attractive" force between the electron and the proton results in their "unity," that is, the birth of the "H" atom. The off product of the "attraction" is "light". As my father, Hazrat Shah Maghsoud Sadegh Angha has said, "Attraction is light and light is attraction." To explain this point, he has said, "Gravitation is actually nothing but attraction between the trapped light of the atoms, i.e., the shared radiation between the electrons and protons." And we read in the Holy Qur'an (24:35):

> "God is the Light of the heavens and the earth. The parable of His Light is as if there were a Niche and within it a Lamp; the Lamp enclosed in Glass: The Glass as it were a brilliant star: Lit from a blessed Tree, an Olive, neither of the East nor of the West, whose oil is well-nigh luminous, Through fire scarce touched it: Light upon Light."

From the foregoing examples, we can see that for anything to come together there must first be attraction. Then harmony, submission and unity are possible. The result is light. This is the key to the teachings of Islam, where the power of attraction creates an internal revolution in the believer, until his entire being is submitted to God, and ultimately he is annihilated in the Absolute, and none remains, but God – 'the Light of the heavens and earth'.

There is only one law in the universe, and that is the law of "Oneness." Knowledge, balance, and harmony are inherent in this law; that is why we see harmony and peace in the universe. Humanity has tried to establish and implement laws, and to devise ideologies and systems – from democracy to Communism – that would make people behave with the same order and balance that we see manifest in the universe. But unfortunately, humanity has not yet been successful. Peace and tranquility have not prevailed in human societies – from the smallest unit, the family, to the global level.

Peace and tranquility can never be realized unless each human being is educated to discover the laws governing his or her being. By education I do not mean "acquired knowledge," but "innate endowed knowledge." We do see educated people who are abusive, who fight and who kill; world leaders who plan wars and order mass executions; and scientists who knowingly and intentionally design weapons of destruction, and so on.

Knowledge manifest in the universe results in stability and peace. The essence of the message of the Prophets has been to teach people how to arrive at the same peace and stability in their own lives. However, instead of practicing these instructions as indicated by the Prophets, people have made religion a matter of inheritance, ritual, and blind faith, which is totally the opposite of what the Prophets have said.

If you do not have knowledge of something, repetition will be of no value. People repeat what the Prophets have said, thinking that they too have the same knowledge. I may know God, and I may tell you that God is real, and that you can see God, and that you can be in communication with God, but this is my experience. Even if you repeat what I say a million times, the experience remains mine and not yours.

If you keep repeating the word knowledge, it will not give you the vast experience contained in the word. Similarly, if you repeat the words peace, stability, and tranquility, you will not have gone through the experience. Therefore, they will not have any reality for you.

Repetition of any word creates images in the mind which are linked to the cultural, social, environmental, political, economic, and etceteras factors, which have shaped the memory files of each individual. For example, if you say "God" to a person who has been reared in a Muslim country or family or environment, his image of God will differ from that of someone who has been brought up in a Jewish or Christian environment. For the Buddhist, the word "God" will have virtually no image. Whereas, if you say "Existence" it will bring images to the person's mind which are directly linked to his or her social, cultural and other environments.

Because all inputs to the brain are a result of the interaction of the senses with the external environment, the information system in the brain, using its data bank stored in the memory files, continuously evaluates incoming information. Based on this process, the brain decides what to do with the incoming information, and then issues its order to the rest of the organs as to what they should do. If the incoming information does not evoke any response in the memory, it is not recognized as valid, unless more detail is provided atop the incoming information, thereby making it possible to connect with what already exists. If it is not reinforced, it is not filed in the long term memory, and eventually it dissipates. In general, whatever we are not familiar with requires more detail so that connection and recognition may take place.

Therefore, knowledge based on the inputs of the senses is limited and not constant. Because the senses are in a state of change, they cannot provide stability and peace. Knowledge based on personal experience and absolute cognition results in peace and tranquility because it is real, since our "being" is in harmony with reality. What ever does not match our "being" or reality becomes a source of conflict and causes stress.

What the Prophets have said is based on knowledge. When you repeat what they have said, it is illusion and it has no reality for you; therefore it becomes a source of conflict. Anything based on knowledge is real. Since imagination is not based on knowledge, but illusion, it does not have a stable foundation and will create stress.

Religion, as practiced in most human societies is not more than illusion. People say, I am a Muslim, Christian, or Jew because they have been born into a Muslim, Christian, or Jewish family. Did the Prophets say you can inherit religion? If the parents' schooling, research, life-experiences can be inherited, so can religion. Can you inherit your parents' experience of love? Or, can you inherit what they had seen in their travels? When we speak about it in such tangible words, it sounds absurd. But, if you pay attention, you will see how absurd it is when people say I am Christian, Jewish, or Muslim, because they had parents who were Christian, Jewish or Muslim.

Just as any action brings with it its own experience, so does religion. Your thirst will not be satisfied if you imagine that you or your parents drink water. When you drink water, your thirst is quenched, your system is released of stress, and then water has a reality for you. You can apply this to all the facets of life.

Religion must have the same reality. This is why Sufism is the reality of religion. It is based on the reality of your "being", the stable and constant center of your existence. It is not imaginary, it cannot be inherited, nor can it be forced, or enforced. Having religion must result in stability in your life at all times, just like the

Prophets. It is not relative and subject to interpretations, whether cultural, environmental, or political.

Each entity in this universe has its source and center of stability. If you look at the evolutionary stages of growth of the fetus you will see that shortly after conception – approximately after twenty-one days – there is a pulse beat, and the mass of cells begin to form into a heart which becomes the life-link and source for the development of the rest of the organism. It is from the heart that the nerves begin to branch out and then the brain and the rest of the organs are formed. The brain and all organs are dependent on the heart throughout their life-cycle. Even at death, it is the heart that works until the last moments of life, whereas, the brain ceases to work as soon as it is cut off from oxygen.

The point of stability and knowledge is the heart in the human being. This is why in the teachings of the Prophets, the heart is so significant. The heart is referred to as the gateway to the unseen, the heavenly kingdom, the *Ka'be*, and so forth. Unfortunately, people have taken the heart to be only a symbolic reference to something beyond. Whereas, it is the physical heart which is the gateway to the realm of God. Hazrat Shah Maghsoud Sadegh Angha, *Pir Oveyssi* has called this luminous point, the source of life in the heart. He

has spoken about this extensively in most of his books including,

The Mystery of Humanity, The Hidden Angles of Life, and *Al-Rasa'el,*

which are available in English, French, Arabic and Persian.

To emphasize this point, I would like to quote a few passages

from the Scriptures and the Holy Qur'an, which point to the

significance of the heart in the teachings of the Prophets:

> "And every wise hearted among you shall come and
> make all the Lord hath commanded." (*Exodus* 35:10)

> "Examine me, O Lord, and prove me; try my reins and
> my heart." (*Psalm of David* 26:2)

> "Have they not traveled in the land, so that they should
> have hearts with which to understand or ears with which
> to hear? For surely it is not their eyes that are blind, but
> blind are the hearts which are in their breasts."
> (*Holy Qur'an* 22:46)

The centrality of the heart in the teachings of the Prophets

is important, because it is the source of our being, and it is to

our source that the return must be made. From the time of the

Upanishads the wise have said: "Know yourself." It is in knowing

yourself that you will be freed of your fears, limitations, and the

false boundaries you have created between yourself, others and

the Existence.

The human being is a complete "book." To read this book, he must learn its alphabet. The Prophets have said, to read our "book," we must return to our origin, to the source of our being. Hazrat Mir Ghotbeddin Mohammad Angha, *Pir Oveyssi* has said:

> "If only the alphabet of the One Spiritual Book were revealed to man, and the secret of the soul discovered, he would need none of the words sealed in silent books, and yet would know the story whole."

The above is the essence of the message of the Prophets. Read your "book," so you may know yourself, so you may know where you came from, why you are here, and what lies beyond your life on earth. All unknowns bring stress, disquiet and instability in our lives. The Prophets have said that each person is capable of discovering the unknowns, and has the knowledge and the means to do this. The source of life in your heart is the way through which you can make this discovery.

Thus, the true meaning of education is learning the alphabet of the book of one's own being, so that we may discover the hidden and unknown dimensions of our being, so our lives may be founded upon knowledge and result in stability and peace.

In my opinion, thinkers and leaders of the world, instead of persisting in designing and implementing an illusory idea known as society, should put aside their past techniques and endeavor to construct a balanced human being and guide him to know his true values. When the true values of one person are totally known, it is possible to design and implement other laws of action that are built upon those values.

In a society where individuals are trained to know their self-worth, that society will enjoy prosperity, happiness and equality, and its members will stand against baseless and unfounded ideas at any cost. They shall know the true meaning of prosperity for the human society, with sound, constructive ideas and actions.

The happiness and prosperity that mankind has envisioned and aspired to for human society will prevail only when all individuals – irrespective of personal disposition, but while enjoying physical well-being –attain and benefit from an elevated spiritual state. A prosperous human society is attained through the outward and inward harmony of each of its members, and their harmonious existence in a unified system.

We must not think that we need to undertake monumental projects to attain this goal. The solution is to discover the stable truth which is common throughout humanity. The human being is the universal system of God evolved from one source. The differences we see among the individual members of humanity are factors added to the human being's pure essence during the course of his evolutionary development in nature and society. The result is that the essence is sacrificed for the sake of its manifestations.

To have stability and peace, we must return to our Source, our Origin. The teachings of the Prophets have provided human beings with a blueprint for this return, so the unknowns which are the source of our uncertainties and instability may be resolved.

May God grant you the resolve to endeavor on the path of self-knowledge; May He teach you the alphabet of the book of the soul so you may read the book of your being; May He grant you patience and perseverance to cultivate your being to its fullest so you will be the peacemakers of your societies; May He open the gate of the City of Knowledge unto your soul, so your actions may be guided by the light of knowledge and wisdom.

ENDNOTES

1. Stark, F. (1992, Dec.) American Institute of Stress. *American Health.* pp. 42-47.

2. Saprio, V. (1994) *Women in American Society.* Mountain View, CA: Mayfield.

3. "Gun Ownership Rises Steadily, And Murder Rate for Young Men Doubles", (1995, Jan. 3) *The Washington Post. Health.* p. 12.

4. Haas, Michael. (1992). A Paradigm of Community for the Post-Cold War World. In Tehranian, Katharine & Majid. (1992). *Restructuring for World Peace.* Creskill, NJ: Hampton Press.

5. Angha, Molana al-Moazam Hazrat Shah Maghsoud Sadegh. (1988). *Al-Rasa'el.* Lanham, MD: University Press of America. p. 14.

6. Al-Rasa'el. p. 16.

7. Al-Rasa'el. p. 21.

8. Barnett, Lincoln. (1961). *The Universe and Dr. Einstein.* New York: William Morrow & Company.

9. Angha, Molana al-Moazam Hazrat Shah Maghsoud Sadegh & Aryainejad, Sirus. (1994). Professor Sadegh Angha's *Theory of Particle Structure and Its Applications (The Epic of Life).* New York: Vantage Press.

SUFISM
AND
WISDOM

In the Name of God,
Most Gracious, Most Merciful

Praise be to God, the summit of perfection and knowledge, the Eternal, the Gracious. He exists, but not by accident, and His existence is not contingent upon anything; He exists, but not from nonexistence. He is with everything, but not in parallel with anything; and He is other than anything but is not separate; He destined the powers and the forces and the heavens, from which He made the seven skies in harmony and balance; within them He placed the sun, the moon, and the stars in their constellations; and everything in the universe, in surrender, forever pulsates to the call of Existence. The night was deemed for knowledge of Him, and the day for the light of His effusions. God's grace be upon His chosen and praised Messenger, Mohammad Mostafa (pbuh), and his pure and innocent followers and successors.

Wisdom and knowledge are words that evoke a sense of inspiration and aspiration, and perhaps awe, in most people. When aligned with Sufism, they become more compelling and to a great extent mystifing. But what do these words really mean? I believe that it is important to demystify things, for them to become accessible and applicable so that everyone may benefit from them; for "the wise attracts benefit and repels loss".[1] I believe this to be the essential function of knowledge.

Having been trained in the discipline of Sufism since childhood, under the guidance of my grandfather and father (the fortieth and the forty-first Masters of Maktab Tarighat Oveyssi Shahmaghsoudi), I have learned that the true scholar is not satisfied with the result of other people's findings, but makes every effort to discover truth for himself. The human quest for knowledge is only valid when its goal is to discover the reality behind the surface value of words, things, entities, etc.

If we take a quick look at the evolutionary process of the various disciplines, we will see that through several thousand years of history, from one single branch called wisdom, thousands of branches have evolved under the headings of science and humanities. If we take a closer look, we will see that the cause of this expansion has been the inquisitive spirit of the human being with its unquenchable thirst to know - an innate drive that doesn't cease to motivate. This urge to know is innate to each human being, irrespective of race, gender, color, religion, etc.

The function of knowledge is to expand, to illuminate, to present, and so forth. The seed bursts open from its shell in order to manifest its knowledge by presenting its roots, stem, leaves, flower and fruit. The sun shines unceasingly; the elements come together and disperse, and come together and disperse again. With each gathering and dispersion, a new manifestation of knowledge is witnessed. Can you point to anything that is not the manifestation of knowledge? Knowledge is absolute!

The human quest for knowledge begins at birth. In reality, it is an urge to return to the Origin, to Knowledge. As I continue speaking, hopefully the meaning of what I have just said will become clear for you. When a child is born, his mental screen is clear. He is born with infinite capabilities and possibilities. From the moment of birth, the infant begins to expand his domain of experience. The fetus in the womb has hands, has eyes, has ears, has all the organs, but does not use them. He has no idea what the sense of touch or taste is like. He has no idea about the visual images he will be encountering, nor the sounds he will be hearing. It doesn't take long before his urge to know prompts him to explore his environment and use the various tools that his innate knowledge had made possible for him during the various phases of growth as a fetus.

As he interacts with his environment, the clear screen of his mind begins to be imprinted with various experiences, forming a back up system with which he begins to assess new incoming information. He then begins to recognize familiar sounds, voices, objects, tastes, etc. As the data increases in the memory files of the brain, more cross references are needed to identify and classify new information, so repeatedly registered information becomes more reinforced and more accessible. Thus, various habits, behavior and thought patterns are formed.

All incoming new information is either accepted or rejected, depending upon whether or not it is in harmony with what already exists. Parents want to give their children what benefits them and makes them comfortable. They want to protect their children from harm. They want to pass on their experiences, feelings, and thoughts to their children -all of which have either been handed down to them by their own parents, or shaped and reshaped by their society, culture and environment - even those concerning religion and God. While one's thoughts may contain some kind of truth, what one receives from the verbal word, or what I call a symbol or contract, does not contain its meaning, even if it creates imaginary references to what it should be.

Now, if I were to come and tell you about God and what I told you did not cross-reference with the image you have in your mind of God, you would either say, "He's crazy", or "He doesn't know." Whereas, if the words that I spoke about God had formed an image in your mind early on, that would be the basis for the measurement of new information. In either case, the information you have collected is invalid and void of knowledge. If you look closely, you will see that your understanding of God was based on what others had described to you, and not your own experience. You had merely accepted what others had said.

The above example can be applied to all unknowns for people. Examples are heaven, hell, eternity, infinity, angels, demons, etc. The meanings of these words are with those who spoke about them, and not with those who blindly repeat them and form images of them in their minds. It is explicitly stated in the *Holy Qur'an* (17:36), "Pursue not that of which you have no knowledge."

How do we distinguish between knowledge, imagination, and illusion? Knowledge is that which we gain through our own personal experience, whereas, illusion is merely giving shape and form to things and events in our minds that have not been our personal experience. Let me clarify that the word experience does not mean repetition. To repeat one thing over and over does not create an experience, it simply reinforces our imagination of that word, whatever that word may be. As an example, I have a dog, and let's say I call him Sam. The word "Sam" has no meaning nor symbolic reference for the dog, but over a period of time, because I keep repeating the name Sam, he will respond. What is he responding to? He is responding to the sound and the tone of my voice, all of which are within the word Sam. This is a contract and not an understanding, nor an experience. Experience is another word for the actualization of knowledge in every aspect of life. It is not an entity that is variable and cannot be accessed and used in time of need.

People think that if they read or hear about things, they also know them. For example, you know what love is, if you have experienced it; you know what sadness is if you have experienced it; you know what joy is if you have experienced it. No matter how much effort I exert in explaining any of the above feelings to you, you will not know what I am talking about unless you have experienced it. Perhaps, you can imagine what I am trying to convey, but the experience of those feelings are not yours. Therefore, those words have no reality for you. We must not forget that, "Words cannot transfer the meaning." [2]

Do you know why there are so many "religions", sects, belief systems, etc.? It is because people's knowledge of God is no more than imagination and illusion. If you and I are both precious gem experts, would we dispute whether or not a pearl is a pearl or a diamond a diamond? Of course not, we would immediately recognize a diamond to be a diamond and not a sapphire or ruby, or whatever else. Would two children who have been reared by the same parents fight with each other about who their parents are? The answer is obvious. Can we assume that the reason for so much religious disputes, hatreds and wars is that God is missing from people's experience?

People think that by reading books, listening to lectures, or following someone blindly, they will know God. If you memorize with total accuracy all the writings of Einstein, will you have his knowledge? Or, if you memorize his formula $E = mc2$, will you have the knowledge that the formula represents, or, if you repeat the formula thousands of times, will you gain access to that knowledge? Or, if I am an excellent writer and scholar, but have no knowledge of physics, and I write a detailed account of the life and works of Einstein, will you think that I have the same knowledge as he?

In physical, tangible matters we do not make such assumptions. If we did, we would be fired, retired, or put away. But, when it comes to issues relating to God, and the message of God, only assumption and illusion are the basis of our understanding. This is why so much superstition surrounds all religious practices. Blind faith is handed down generation after generation, taking the color of the environment, culture, geographical and ethnic conditions of people. Religion has become no more than a commodity, transacted for various purposes and goals.

But what is the essence of the teachings of the Prophets, how is it related to Sufism, and what is its relevance for today? If we look objectively and with sincerity at the lives and teachings of the Holy Prophets, it will be very clear that their lives were devoted to announcing, and sharing with others, their unique discovery. The method through which they had arrived at their discovery was not because of what others had said before them, nor because they feared or trusted someone. Instead, they had an innate unquenchable urge to "know" which could not be satisfied except through personal experience.

Like the Prophets, true scientists devote their life to study and research, and whenever they make a discovery, they see it as their duty to announce it for the benefit and welfare of humanity. They do not force others to accept, nor do they ask people to accept blindly what they have said. They invite the scientific community to go through the same process of research and discovery as they had, so they may also arrive at the same results. The Prophets have always said, validate what we are saying through your own experience, so you may discover the truth for yourself.

Hazrat Shah Maghsoud Sadegh Angha, in his book *Dawn*, has explained this very clearly. He states that the Prophets appeared at a time when people were worshipping idols. The Prophets told the people that the idols they had created with their own hands were limited, and not worthy of worship. They told them that they knew God, they were in communication with God, and that what they told them were His words. They said, God had given these directions, so they might act on these words, and know Him, and not worship idols. [3]

What people did and still do, is take the words of the Prophets and cross reference them with what exists in their memory files, and imagine God accordingly. Is this the God the Prophets were speaking about? Is this god great, and worthy of worship? Is it not less worthy than the idols of the past?

The essence of the message of the Prophets is that each person must individually cognize God in his or her being. God cannot be known through what He has said, or what others say. This is philosophy – un-validated knowledge – whereas, the knowledge of the Prophets is validated through personal experience or absolute cognition.

We never accept that a child has knowledge of medicine because his parents are physicians, but we say we are Muslims, Jews, Christians, etc. because we were born into a family who are Muslims, Jews, or Christians. Isn't this absurd? How can we justify such ignorance? Can you inherit such knowledge genetically, or environmentally?

Knowledge of the Prophets is the knowledge of absolute existence; therefore it is vast and eternal. Whereas, knowledge acquired through sensory perception registered and processed in the brain is limited. The brain functions much like a computer. It works according to the program it is given, and cannot go beyond that. Its input frequency and output response change with the addition of new information. The brain is the organizer, the manager, and the commander of the body. Its function is to operate this machinery to its optimum capacity and protect it from danger. Its mode of operation doesn't exceed this. It is nurtured by nature, and it interacts with nature. The realm of nature is forever changing and nothing is constant. The cycles of nature, the evolutionary changes of living organisms, or the life cycles of beings, are evident examples of this.

If we were to agree on the definition of truth as being that which "exists and is constant," [4] then we would realize the significance of the message of the Prophets. The infinite cannot be known through the limited - the senses and the brain are limited.

One of the basic principles of Sufism is that you cannot know anything that is outside of you, because to know something in its totality requires that you be that entity. Since our recognition of things is based on contracts and our understanding of those symbols, and because our feelings keep shifting and our senses are continuously activated, we cannot know anything outside of ourselves. Therefore, the best place to look for the answers to our being is right within the unbounded reality of ourselves. In this context, each person is the researcher, the laboratory, and the subject of study.

Perhaps if I explain the different levels of the human being, you will more readily understand what I have just said. The human being consists of the following four levels:

The outermost level is the level of nature, which is the laboratory for human experience.

The second level is the physiological level, the cellular, organic level which functions according to its own inherent programs and laws. The activities of this level are generally a combination of sensory activities, thought, cellular needs, and experiences, as well as cultural heritage and personal aptitudes. Medical science focuses on this level and its useful technological and treatment advances have dealt with aspects of the cellular, organic level.

The third level is the developmental level, the locus for mental, sensory and psychic powers and for the development and interrelationship of the magnetic bodies.

The fourth level is the innermost level, the mysterious level, which is the point of stability and true personality. Amir al-Mo'menin Ali (peace be upon him) said, "Do you think you are an insignificant germ? The greater world lies within you." This is the level which is the source of knowledge as announced by the Prophets, and the focus of the teachings of Maktab Tarighat

Oveyssi Shahmaghsoudi.

Each level of the human being has its own sphere of operation and is submitted to the laws governing it. The instructions of the Prophets are meant to acquaint people with all the levels of their being, their interaction and relationship with the extensive universe, and the laws governing their being, so they may live in peace and tranquility and know their eternity.

The Holy Prophet Mohammad (pbuh) has said, "Knowledge is not obtained through scholarship, but it is a light that God shines in the heart of whom He wills." As mentioned earlier, the function of knowledge is to dispel ignorance and illuminate the darkness.

The Prophets, Saints, and the Enlightened have always shared with the people of their time the ways and means of how they attained their wisdom and knowledge. They have said that humans are ignorant of their true identity and their true human right. They have said that humans live in darkness. Their definition of the human being far exceeds those provided by various theoretical and scientific disciplines. They see humans caged in the boundaries of limitation that are self created. The Prophets see humans in this manner. They see humans burdened and anchored to limitation because of their attachments, needs, prejudices, biases, etc.

The materialistic attachments, and their influence, create solid boundaries for people in which they become trapped - prisoners of ignorance and self-inflicted bondage. The essential message of the Prophet is that: You are created free. Know your true dignity and your eternity. However, the identity people formulate for themselves is based on what their society, family, culture and country provide for them, which they unconsciously obey, without knowledge.

People's basis for measuring who they are and their self-worth are these changeable social and cultural factors. In contrast, the Prophet Mohammad (pbuh) has said, "Whoever cognizes their true self, has cognized God."

In Islam, the dignity assigned to the true personality of humans is no other than the Divine. Sufism is a discipline, a method and a way that teaches humans how to attain their true state of dignity as stated by the Prophets. Therefore, Sufism is the reality of religion. Sufism is the method through which the Prophets attained the cognition of God, and their true self and personality.

The accurate word for Sufism is *Irfan*, derived from the Arabic word *ma'rifa,* meaning to cognize, to know. When can we say we know something? It is when nothing about the subject of inquiry remains unknown to us. Perhaps, the best way to describe Sufism is to say, it is the School of Self Knowledge. It teaches its students to discover their hidden talents and abilities; expand their perception; break the boundaries of limitation; and ultimately journey through the heavens of their being.

My father, Hazrat Shah Maghsoud Sadegh Angha, *Pir Oveyssi,* in his book, *The Principles of Faghr and Sufism,* has said that the human being is not a mass of cells, but an intricate weave of the heavens and the earth in whom lies all potential - from the beast to that surpassing the angels, from darkness to light. In essence, the human being has a choice as to where and what he wants to be in this intricate and infinite fabric of Existence. He has further said, "When nature wanted to manifest itself in its most subtle of forms, it became an entity called the human being." [5]

Just as the physical sciences have endeavored to know the physical aspects of the human being, the social scientists have endeavored to know his motivations, and the reasons for his behaviors and actions. With all the sophisticated research, the human being still remains a mystery to them. Essentially, all of their efforts are geared towards facilitating human life on earth, by making advances in technology and agriculture, and by manipulating nature and the genetic codes.

What remains hidden from their sphere of study is the "I" who is the doer behind all investigation, search, and action. Who is the "I" that does not cease to voice its presence from the moment of birth, and remains constant throughout life, although everything else goes through the cycle of change? Islam gives such a high rank to the human being, that it leaves no separation between "I" and God. This is the wisdom and knowledge of the Prophets.

The way to self-knowledge begins with an innate urge on the part of the seeker who genuinely wants to know the reason for his being, becoming and the hereafter. In other words, he finds himself between two unknowns – where he came from, and where he will go. He is seeking answers that are not available through the investigative and theoretical disciplines.

The Prophet of Islam has said, "I am the city of Knowledge, and Ali is its door." Entering the realm of God requires the presence of a teacher who has been inwardly introduced to the seeker by God.

In the Holy Qur'an (57:9) it is stated, "He is the One Who sends to His servant manifest Signs, that He may lead you from the depths of darkness into the Light." And, (57:17) "Already have We shown the Signs plainly to you, that ye may learn wisdom."

To attain the state of wisdom and knowledge, the seeker must go through the seven states of transformation and purification under the guidance of the *Pir* (Spiritual Teacher), who has been inwardly revealed by God. The seven states reflect the process through which the seeker (*Salek*) begins to move from the external to the internal; from a state of dependency on the external to a state of inward stability; from a state of agitation to a state of tranquility; from a state of being needy to a state of fulfillment; from a state of limitation to a state of discovery and expansion.

These states reflect the changes that take place. For example, being in control of all natural appetites, desires, and dependencies (emotional, physical, etc.), the seeker begins to feel an inward release and a sense of freedom and peace. The constant external attractions that had pulled him in different directions no longer control him.

As the seeker puts into practice the instructions he has received from the Pir - prayers, fasting, meditation, and *zekr* (remembrance of God) - the realm of the heart and soul become accessible to him. He begins the journey to the hidden and mysterious realm of his being. It is during these times of spiritual elevation that the seeker transcends the boundaries of time and place and enters the state of witnessing and cognition which are inaccessible to the senses.

The seeker's ultimate goal is to dissolve in the Absolute Truth - God. The directions and instructions he receives from the Pir are to guide him to reach the stage of cognition as stated in the *Holy Qur'an* (24:37), "Men whom neither traffic nor merchandise can divert from the remembrance of God, nor from regular Prayer". Bayazid Bastami, a disciple of Imam Ja'far Sadegh (peace be upon him) has said, "No other but God is within my robe." [6]

As you can see from the above, Sufism is a discipline, a system of education that transforms humans from their base state, to their divine state. Each of the stages brings with it a change, a revolution and evolution for the seeker.

During this process of transformation and training, the seeker's awareness expands as he develops the subtle dimensions hidden within him. For example, one of the keys to progress toward this realization is *zekr* (remembrance). The formal rendition of *zekr* is in prayer and in chants. Both include the *zekr* of words, *zekr* of movement of the body, and *zekr* of heart. It is a process of purification of the heart, of cleansing and releasing. In the stages of *zekr*, first all is relinquished, then he who is witnessing the Presence forgets the *zekr*, and thirdly, he shall no longer see himself, but only the Divine Beloved, "All that is on earth will perish: But will abide (for ever) the Face of thy Lord." (Holy Qur'an, 55:26,27).

My grandfather, Hazrat Mir Ghotbeddin Mohammad Angha, in his book, From Fetus to Paradise: The Evolutionary States of Man, has said:

> "Bird of paradise I am,
> To this earth I belong not.
> This body's been made a cage
> Just for a few brief days. """

There are many layers connecting the physical body to the spiritual realm. These levels are directly connected to the electromagnetic centers existing in different locations in the human being, each serving a specific function as well as working in a continuous relationship with the various organs and glands. There are thirteen main electromagnetic centers and numerous minor ones. The main center is located in the heart, and has been called by my father, *"the source of life in the heart."*[8] This center

is very important in the teachings of the School of Islamic Sufism.

Amir al-Mo'menin Ali (peace be upon him) has said, "The heart is

an open book."

The return to the origin, of which I spoke earlier, refers to this

center in the heart. A brief period after conception (twenty-one

days), a pulsation occurs in the mass of cells, and from this point

the heart begins to form. After the heart is formed, the nerves begin

to branch out and ultimately the brain and the other parts evolve.

The heart is the seat of knowledge in the teachings of Sufism.

This is why meditation in the heart is so crucial and important. It is

returning to the source of our being, the source of knowledge and

our true identity.

The first layer beyond the physical body which the seeker

becomes familiar with, is the etheric body. This is the template or

mold for the physical body. This spiritual body has a spiritual heart

which is hidden behind the physical heart. The "secret or hidden

heart", as it is known in the Sufi tradition, is directly connected

with the existential healing powers. The spiritual heart transmits

spiritual energy which forms a body embracing the physical body.

This etheric or corporeal body is adapted to the palpable world. It is the origin of the body's electrical current, which is transmitted from the spiritual heart to the physical heart. Disconnection of this power from the heart will cause the heart to stop beating. The etheric body vanishes two or three days after the soul separates from the body.

The second body is the celestial or astral body. This body is more delicate, and is situated over the etheric body. It originates in the heavenly celestial world and is the communication link with the spiritual world.

The third body is the rational body. It is even more delicate, luminous and transparent than the celestial body. Revelation and inspiration originate from this body. Seekers are guided by the souls of Prophets, Saints and the Enlightened to the celestial sphere through this body. They also inspire luminous thoughts and divine ideas in the hearts of truth seekers.

The fourth body is the luminous body, sometimes called the fire halo. This body is responsible for the ascension of the rational soul to the spiritual world. The soul of man can only attain this position through great patience and devotion. Those souls which sacrifice themselves to serve others with a fervent love will form a luminous halo, similar to the halo around the moon. This is the luminous halo painted around the heads of the Prophets and Saints.

Any true system of education is supposed to dispel ignorance. The principles of Sufism, based on the pillars of Islam, are a set of instructions intended for the serious student who wishes to discover his or her reality, which result in freedom, stability and knowledge. These results cannot be attained through blind faith, rituals, trust, hallucination, repetition, or whatever is handed down from parents, society, and culture. Unfortunately, as in all "religious practices", it is not uncommon to see the teachings of Sufism reduced to no more than ritualistic practices appealing to the imagination of people, void of reality. The Prophet Mohammad (pbuh) has said, "Faith is not achieved for the asking, but settles in the heart and is confirmed by actions."

Would anyone who has undergone the training and transformation described above, steal, murder, hate, hoard, kill, rape, or abuse? The answer is evident. If we separate the prevalent religious teachings and practices from the essence of the message of the Prophets it will be clear why religion has lost its dignity and value in the lives of people. Unless human nature is transformed; unless people become acquainted with and begin to experience their more subtle and tender levels of being, societies will not change, and aggression, hatred, and killings will continue to devastate human lives.

Religion in its true sense is not only for the benefit of the individual, but also for the health and welfare of society, as well as stability in nature.

I have endeavored today, to present to you to the greatest extent possible, the knowledge underlying the message of the Prophets, whose reality is presented and taught in the School of Islamic Sufism - the School of Self-Knowledge. Perhaps those who are susceptible of heart and mind have heard my words, and will act upon them to bridge the alienation that has evolved through the ages between religion and knowledge. Perhaps, those of you who are receptive will want to explore and discover the reality of your own being, to find out for yourself the truth of the message of the Prophets.

If my words have touched one single soul today I know I will have done my duty as ordained by the Lord of believers, the God of the heavens and earth.

May God grant you the wisdom of Socrates, so you may confess your ignorance before the infinite Existence. May He grant you the gifts he bestowed upon His chosen: abstention from Abraham, remembrance from Moses, fasting from Jesus, annihilation and subsistence in God from Mohammad (pbuh), and a thirst with which you will endeavor on the path of Self-Knowledge, excavating the treasures of your being and reaping their benefits for the health, happiness, and prosperity of yourself, your family, society, country, and the world.

The Holy Prophet Mohammad (pbuh) has said, "The human being is like a mine gold, silver, or jewel - excavate their goodness, so you may have peace."

ENDNOTES

1. Angha, Hazrat Shah Maghsoud Sadegh. (1989). *Dawn*. Lanham, MD: University Press of America, p. 25

2. *Dawn*. p. 30

3. *Dawn*. pp. 17-18.

4. *Dawn*. p. 25.

5. Angha, Hazrat Shah Maghsoud Sadegh. *The Principles of Faghr & Sufism*. (1987). Verdugo City CA: M.T.O. Shahmaghsoudi Publications. p. 10.

6. Angha, Hazrat Shah Maghsoud Sadegh. (1986). *Al-Rasa'el*. Lanham, MD: University Press of America. p. 19

7. Angha, Hazrat Mir Ghotbeddin Mohammad. (1987). *Az Janin ta Janan (From Fetus to Paradise: The Evolutionary States of Man)*. Verdugo City, CA: M.T.O. Shahmaghsoudi® Publications. p. 22.

8. Angha, Hazrat Shah Maghsoud Sadegh. (1986). *The Mystery of Humanity: Tranquility and Survival*. Lanham, MD: University Press of America.

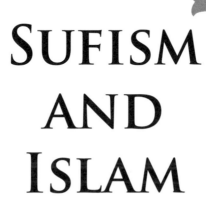

SUFISM
AND
ISLAM

In the Name of God, Most Gracious, Most Merciful

Praise to the All Merciful Lord who has manifested the universe,

upon the wisdom of the Holy Qur'an. He then created man to sustain

cognition and to declare that wisdom through faith and submission.

Praise to the "One" who expands unity to encompass all beings,

who nurtures truth in the midst of all expression, and who grants

enlightenment to his worshippers' early morning pleas.

In adherence to the blessed command of God in the *Holy Qur'an*

(57:7), "And spend (in charity) out of the (substance) whereof He

has made you Heirs", it is my intention to express the essence

of metaphysical revelations and scientific explorations using the

simplest explanations. In accord with the laws of nature which

guide every single sound wave to its awaiting capable receiver,

may the truth of these teachings find their expectant receivers and

transcend the barriers of time, place, language, prejudice, and

superstition. May this conveyance of understanding demolish

the wall of misinterpretation and ignorance that has separated physical and metaphysical sciences. May the true seeker find his way to the ultimate truth freely, without the bondage of blind faith, superstition, preconceived bias or supposition.

"Irfan", or Sufism, reveals itself through time; in each era, in its own unique way. It is neither confined by words nor restrained by social customs. It is the practical approach to "gnosis" which means knowledge of "Self". The School of Islamic Sufism provides the path to recognizing one's true "Self", preventing one from going astray by showing how materialistic bonds and attachments prevent humans from experiencing the more elevated states of their existence.

In this brief presentation, my purpose is to present the true meaning of one or two topics, i.e. to expand on the reality of these topics rather than relying on assumed social definitions.

In this era, especially with the advent of instantaneous global communication, the metaphysical sciences are perceived as mythical or superfluous pastimes. Most people perceive the teachings of the Prophets in this inept manner. If the views which are presented differ somewhat from their own preconceived ideologies, they are interpreted as fanatic or backward. If their main interest is politics and economics, then they are likely to interpret religious beliefs as a source of demonic actions and terrorism. Such superficial interpretations have led to the fabrication of new "religions" as a means of supporting the political and economic demands of a particular group or to cover the ignorance of another. Such manufactured "religions", and their references to historic, poetic and mystical anecdotes have become the criteria for acceptance or rejection of God's teachings.

The traditional way of presenting a topic is to express an idea using terminology which seems familiar, but whose truth has not yet been revealed. By using such terminology or repeating the interpretations of famous philosophers, past or present, the speaker ultimately seeks to impose his views on the audience or gain their acceptance. This brings to mind the example of a child's composition in which the student expounds on the topic of "spring" using his own unattained wishes and dreams, repeating others' quotations, and drawing a picture of "spring" based on what was in his mind. Needless to say, the spring that nature presents is far different from that which is described by the child.

To comprehend the essence of a topic, one needs to return and refer to its origin, and not to the marginal notes surrounding it. He who experiences thirst seeks water, and is not concerned with the container. If a man is hungry, he strives to find food, and is not distracted by the plate or the garnishments. If one suffers from an ailment, one searches for the cure, and does not focus on the mood of the physician or the taste of the medicine. Likewise, if a person is attempting to gain knowledge in a field of science, it should be the essence of that knowledge and the humanitarian outcome of it that must be foremost in his mind, and not the social status and financial gain it may offer. Such must be the devotion of one who is a seeker of the truth and the reality of existence. He must also return and refer to the existence itself, instead of philosophical arguments, mystical stories, superficial traditions, social customs or socio-economic, political propaganda & aspirations.

> "Principles that are used in limitation are not the means
> for the discovery of the infinite."[1]

A brief look at the course of science throughout history shows that there was once a time when all sciences were studied together and were collectively called "wisdom". The interested student could study biology, mathematics, and the metaphysical sciences simultaneously. There was a generality in "wisdom" that any researcher who could gather any degree of information, however deficient, could focus upon and address. Since this approach did not produce any real solutions, there was a gradual change starting about 3000 years ago. During the time of Democritus, Socrates, Plato, and finally Aristotle, the debates and conflict of ideas resulted in the expansion of science from an abstract form to a detailed one. Hence, in our present period, each science has branched out into specialized research fields.

Scholars and scientists of physics and its derivatives attempt to discover the governing laws of nature and the hidden capacities of particles, in order to facilitate and optimize the living conditions of man.

Biologists study organisms and by unveiling each membrane and each layer of the manifestations of existence, attempt to gain a glimpse of the source of life. They have broken the genetic code of many organisms and are trying to read the human genetic code. By accessing the genetic instructions for the formation of organisms, they seek to reprogram and reshape their properties and traits in ways that will most benefit mankind. Be it for pharmaceutical, medical, nutritional, or other objectives, scientists are seeking and finding ways to optimally utilize whatever nature has offered.

Researchers in the field of psychology and its related branches attempt to observe and define a person's behaviors and reactions as a social entity. In trying to understand thought processes of the mind, they aspire to improve the dynamics of relationships between people, thus making them better suited for society.

These and many other fields of science resemble different branches of a tree. Although each branch presents its own growth and has a place of its own, there is one trunk from which they all grow and there was one seed that opened itself into this magnificent presentation.

In the study of all sciences, it is the reality of man's "self" which is forever seeking, searching in curiosity, with that inward vision and quest for knowledge which is the seed of all sciences. The driving force behind man's quest for revealing the hidden truth beneath the disguises and for surpassing the limitations forced upon him by nature, is his inherent, infinite identity. It is that innate "I" who searches and researches everything from a particle to the universe, embracing all knowledge that is to be discovered. So, the origin and source of all sciences, physical or metaphysical, is the self or

"I". It is not any wonder that therein also resides the ultimate goal and purpose of all these researches and scientific explorations.

What is "*Irfan*" (Sufism)? It is the path to knowing this "true self". It is cognition of this entity in its absolute form, with all its attributes and capabilities. This is the reality of religion and the essence of God's teachings conveyed through the Prophets. This is "*Irfan*"! The Holy Prophet Mohammad (pbuh) has said in the *Nahj-ol Fissaha*, "Knowledge is not in the skies to descend upon you, nor is it in the earth to grow for you, but it is hidden within you."

Clearly, this is the reason for the importance of Sufism in the progress and ultimate achievements of science. Unless the human being is recognized in his totality as an absolute being, with all of his capacities in every stage of his existence, all efforts to discover and capture the hidden aspects of nature will be deemed insufficient and deficient.

Just as the process for properly using and displaying a jewel is to first discover its true value by removing all the layers of dirt and impurities, then sculpting it so that the sun is reflected from each and every angle. In the same manner, the human being must find his own true "value", his inherent identity. He too must remove all earthly bonds that imprison his soul, purify from all impurities,

and free himself of all material attributes such as his environment,

his society, his possessions, his thoughts, his needs, etc. Only after

purification of "I" from whatever else there is, can we achieve

cognition. This is the only way to provide the perfect surroundings

and environment for the true human being.

Molana Shah Maghsoud Sadegh Angha has said in *The Principles*

of Faghr and Sufism:

> "The human being in its varying completeness of
> physical and metaphysical aptitudes can be defined from
> the savage and beastly level of his primitive ancestors, to
> the level of intellectuals, discoverers, researchers, to the
> rank of gnostics and to the exalted state of prophethood,
> and to the state of annihilation and eternal existence in
> God. That is to say, what degree and rank, and what
> stage of innate individual stability he has reached,
> which in effect reflect the characteristics of that genuine
> capability at the stage of individual talent.
>
> The gravest error would be to classify the vast and
> noble realm of the human being, like other creatures,
> in the framework of limited thoughts – physical
> form, environmental needs and changing nature –
> when, his ascending and noble rank which is drawn
> in Existence, consists of various stages starting from
> humanity (*insaniat*) to (*adamiat*) divinity. The universe
> presented before the human being, which in scientific
> measurements is infinite, is the perceived image of his
> own inner infinite existence."[2]

This is why the teachings of *Irfan* (Sufism), which is the reality of religion, are free of superficial interpretations, suppositions, ignorance, and blind faith. All of which unfortunately, appear to be the building blocks and driving forces of most churches, mosques, and synagogues.

The word *Irfan* means gnosis. This concept has been used in the mathematical, biological, and physical sciences, indicating in-depth research into the reality of each subject. For instance, when the phrase "mathematical gnosis" is used, it means that the researcher has stepped beyond the ordinary boundaries of mathematics and is seeking to find the reality of it. But the definition of gnosis particularly refers to religious gnosis. The *arif* (Sufi) is he who has attained knowledge of the reality of religion. If the purpose of scientific work is to reveal the truth that is hidden and illuminate the meaning of life, we can logically conclude that science and *Irfan* (Sufism) are the same.

It is apparent that if someone does a vast amount of work researching the life and accomplishments of a mathematician, even if his research is entirely accurate, detailed, and as close to reality as possible, no one would call the researcher a mathematician. It is of utmost importance that we realize that the same is true in the metaphysical sciences. Even if someone studies the classical forms of *Irfan*, researches the life of the Sufis, and writes extensive volumes regarding the philosophy, writings, and lifestyles of those Sufis, he himself has not attained the state of self cognition, and the title of Sufi would be false and inaccurate for him.

The same analogy can be used to clarify another misunderstood point which might otherwise mislead an eager seeker of truth. It is clear that repeating Einstein's equation expressing relativity (E=mc2) as many times as possible, or chanting or proclaiming it, would not lead the speaker to experience the state of realization and discovery attained by Einstein. A person who merely repeats the teachings of the Prophets, or uses the philosophy and terminology of Sufism, cannot achieve the state of enlightenment, nor will he experience cognition. He would be lacking the wisdom and knowledge of the Sufi.

As inept and facetious as it seems, if we observe our own attitude and behavior toward metaphysical subjects, it becomes apparent that this is exactly the behavior we engage in. People may pretend to know about existence, gnosis, and the meaning of life, but their lifestyles indicate they are far from cognition. The only thing they recognize as the state of "enlightenment" is their philosophical arguments and undefined vocabulary. "Knowledge based on physical observation is the greatest veil in the discovery of truth."[3]

Another factor which may prevent a seeker from attaining higher levels of revelation and discovery in both metaphysical and physical sciences is substitution of other people's acquisitions and discoveries in place of personal and inherent insight and creativity. In one of his interviews Albert Einstein stated: "It is almost a miracle that modern teaching methods have not entirely strangled the holy curiosity of inquiry".[4]

It is unfortunate that a faulty system of education is forcing eager students to spend most of their time memorizing and repeating the findings of great men of science. Instead they could be encouraged to refer to and seek their own identity and to present their personal creativity. Unless it is clarified for the seeker that the discoveries and teachings of esteemed scholars, past or present, must only be used as an introduction, a stepping stone to his own research and inquiry, he may be doomed to a destiny of forever carrying in his mind the work and ideas of others, unaware of his own potentials.

He would resemble a spring of water which has accumulated excessive debris on its fountainhead. Soon, the water that is held back and blocked will become stagnant and lose its ability to give refreshment and life. This is why it is constantly emphasized to the seeker that memorizing and carrying other people's ideologies and revelations will cause hindrance and impede him on his journey of self-cognition.

The *Salek* is a seeker who transcends the various stages in his journey to discover the truth. Through repentance he returns from the path of disunity and absorption in desires. He has taken his life, back to heaven; the totality and unity of his true identity. In this journey each layer of earthly bondage is removed and the seeker experiences and resides in the ultimate state of tranquility and harmony.

Practical Sufism is based on conscious awareness: that which is inherent and pure in every human being. Philosophical Sufism is based on deduction and reasoning of the mind. The seeker who practices Sufism learns to control and stop the chattering of his mind in order to eliminate mental deductions, illusions, and imaginings that have no relevance to the truth of his being. This is the only way to experience reality in its true form.

Philosophical Sufism uses sensory perceptions, thought processes, and mental deductions. It is therefore limited to the relative comparisons of things, a process which is far from absolute. Since reality is beyond the scope of limited sensory perceptions, comparisons and the conventional arrangements that we create in our minds, it is emphasized to the seeker that on this journey he should concentrate and meditate. This results in controlling the senses and stops the wanderings of the mind.

As was mentioned earlier, the basis and source of science is the inquiring soul, that creative "self" which breaks through the mind's limitations and steps beyond the social and cultural norms in order to discover the unknown. Sufism is the cognition of this inquisitive soul and the creative self. Sufism is the essence of religion and the reality of the teachings of the Prophets. It is neither based on interpretations nor blind faith. The true meaning of science is the discovery of truth and the genuine application of all the creative forces within the human being, above and beyond that which is interpreted by others.

Therefore, it seems obvious that to achieve an all-encompassing success, one must utilize science and Sufism together. The seeker, an individual who has risen in search of truth, seeking to experience the reality of it, resembles a bird who needs the two wings. Those wings are science and Sufism, working in harmony and stability, to experience flying in the kingdom of "self".

Thus, it is clear that exploration and cognition of truth requires a return from the level of philosophy and words which are the domain of comprehension, to the state of truth, which is the realm of revelation. As God states in the *Holy Qur'an*, "Everything will perish but His Face." (28:88), "Thus seek the path leading to Allah." (9:20)

It is essential for the researcher to unveil the hidden and eliminate any uncertainty. The seeker is he who reveals reality and establishes himself within it. Then the truth in all its aspects and angles is uncovered. He becomes the knowledgeable one, or as it is sometimes said, enlightened. As it is stated in the *Holy Qur'an*: "When the Event Inevitable cometh to pass."(56:1) "And verily Judgment and Justice must indeed come to pass." (51:6)

It may be necessary at this point to expand on the meaning of what has already been discussed, and explain the meaning of the words that will follow. For instance, let us examine the words, "comprehend" and "comprehension". What is meant by comprehension is an explanation of something as perceived by our senses, an elaboration of its reflected image engraved in the brain. Relative comparisons between these man-made images result in comprehension. Revelation is not based on constructed images and limited perceptions, therefore one cannot use comparisons with it. Comprehension is a series of actions and reactions that are derived from external observations of an object. Whatever we comprehend by observing an object is something that is recognizable by our senses. For example, the sun – we encounter its activity, but this is not the reality of the sun. We cannot comprehend the distance, the actual heat, or the size of it. The instruments man uses to comprehend are his five senses, his mind, his memory, and whatever symbolic image is preserved in his brain as a result of repetitious encounters. What's more, this process is not based on one's own creativity, choice, or will, but rather one's comprehension of subjects is derived from what one's society, family, traditions, and ideologies of the past have constructed.

Words, commentaries, and the conventional methods we use, as useful as they are, remain completely insufficient as the means of recognizing the truth.

> "To receive spiritual truths and to cognize the spiritual stages, one cannot depend upon reason which is rooted in matter." [5]

As long as research is focused on the surface or layers of the subject under study, the results in both the physical and metaphysical sciences will be incomplete, superficial and unreliable. True research is attained when the researcher explores and discovers all aspects of a subject where not even one point or angle is excluded from his observation.

This is why knowledge of each and every single manifestation of life, of which there is an infinite number and unlimited variety, is not a logical approach to cognition of existence. There is layer after layer to be removed and always more veils to be uncovered. It seems logical to conclude that in order to gain knowledge of existence, human beings should concentrate and focus on cognizing (knowing) each and every aspect of the only manifestation of life that is truly available to them, and that is one's own "self".

Our relationship with the external world is based on our limited sensory inputs and self-made thought processes. Sensory receptors with their bounded range only accept certain wavelengths and frequencies translated into a series of action potentials which is the language of the brain. This translation process is affected by the observer's physical and emotional condition, mood, etc. This is then stored in the brain and is based on a series of variables, which results in a perception that is nothing but one's own creation. This illusion is far from the reality of that object. This is why if one cuts an apple in half and gives one half to one person and the other half to another, the first one may describe his share of the apple as sour, while the other one claims the same apple is sweet. Is the apple sweet or sour? Neither! The reality of an apple is situated within the apple, and it is not bound to comparisons. No one can recognize that reality no matter how much research is done on the characteristics of the apple. As long as the observer and that which is being observed are separated, the reality remains hidden. As Molana Shah Maghsoud Sadegh Angha has said, "We do not really hear the special tune of things, but the tune that we do hear is the tune of our own soul."[6]

So, whatever exists has specific characteristics of its own, and can neither cognize nor present anything other than itself. For example, when the word "water" is expressed, it specifies certain characteristics which are only manifested in water. Although the reality it contains is inherently absolute, as soon as it is presented in a physical form and bounded to a certain state of existence, it exhibits a particular appearance reflecting characteristics of its own. The same holds true for each of us. Existence is infinite and absolute. The basis and inherent component of existence in each creature, whatever form and shape it takes, is true reality and being, which transcribes unity and singularity. To gain knowledge of this inherent reality and absolute unity, one cannot focus his research outside of himself. This is why the guiding rule that illuminates the path of all seekers from the smallest particle to far reaching galaxies is expressed in this teaching of Maktab Tarighat Oveyssi Shahmaghsoudi:

> "Nothing but darkness is what lies outside of you,
> And nothing but light is what lies within you."

If the path of discovery is limited to superficial observation of external objects, the result will not be accurate nor will it provide the all encompassing truth which would satisfy the inquisitive soul of the seeker. It is essential for the investigator to search the depth of his own true "self", where illuminated by the light within, he will transcend to the state of gnosis and discover the truth of life.

The investigator who has gained knowledge of the reality of his own existence, has discovered religion. Thus there is no longer any doubt or hesitation. In other words, he has now established his life on the stable basis that is his true "self", which is the only true reality and is completely free of doubt and hesitation. As it is stated in the *Holy Qur'an* (2:1-3):

> "Alif Lam Mim. This is the Book; in its guidance there is no doubt for the devout. Those who believe in the Unseen, Are steadfast in their prayer, And give of what We have Provided for them."

This is why Prophets and the Holy Saints persistently guide man to the path of self knowledge. As Imam Ali (peace be upon him) has said:

> "Do you not ponder that you are a microcosm? And contained within you is the macrocosm? And you are that Clear Book whose words reveal the hidden."[7]

The Holy Prophet Mohammad (peace and blessings upon him) has said:

> "Whoever cognizes the true self has cognized God."

One of the teachings of Socrates which was engraved on the entrance to his school was: "Know thy self." And as Hazrat Mir Ghotbeddin Mohammad Angha has said:

"It became evident that my Beloved was inside the house,
All external search was nothing but idle talk and a trap"[8]

It is essential to evaluate man in the various levels of existence

as he is the focus of all thought and interaction. Basically, man can

be evaluated on two levels, the materialistic and the spiritual. The

first includes three levels:

1.   The materialistic nature where physical interactions with

     the external world take place;

2.   The physical body which provides physiological and

     mechanical functions; and

3.   Finally, the delicate physical body which is nurtured by

     either the materialistic or spiritual dimensions.

The spiritual dimension contains the core of one's being and one's

true identity. Each state provides its own distinct and particular

result, varying from each other. To know man, one should study

him in all these dimensions and levels. Imam Ja'far Sadegh (peace

be upon him) has said:

> "The manifestation of man is God's greatest proof for
> his creatures, for he is a book which has been created
> by His wisdom; he is the totality of all that exists; the
> straight path to all that is good, and the bridge which is
> drawn between heaven and hell."

For the sake of clarification, let us use the metaphor of man as a comet. His true identity is the fiery core which resembles the source of its creation. This is the heaven promised by the Prophets. The layers close to the core contain varying degrees of light, and the outer most layer is dark and in total contrast to the core. This is the materialistic nature, also referred to as hell. Hell is the unstable part of man which is in constant change, filled with demands and desires, and which is never satisfied. One who spends his life building and tending this unstable materialistic nature, satisfying each and every desire, is spending his days in darkness and ignorance. He will not benefit from the light of knowledge that is within him; and of his inherent and infinite ocean of capacities and capabilities, he would only benefit but a drop.

The reality of religion is an invitation to the journey from without to within; a transcendence from the stages of dispersion and disunity to the state of boundless unity. It is the transition from the darkness of ignorance to the light of knowledge, from hell to heaven. The more one becomes entrenched in the various layers and stages that separate his limited, materialistic form from his infinite, absolute being, the more difficult it will be to become free and detached and capable of rising up to fulfill this journey.

This is why the seeker is reminded to be persistent in gathering all his energy in the focal point within him, and to repent from wasting his energy on the external world. If we pay close attention to the pattern of growth in a child, it becomes apparent that at the time of birth and for awhile thereafter, the child is compelled to spend energy in order to establish relative conformity with the world around him. This expenditure of energy through the senses allows him to gain a sense of coordination and relative adaptation with the outside world. Whether it is done out of habit or in order to achieve complete adaptation, that person who is constantly living in his external world is bound by desires and wishes. He is constantly trying to adapt himself to his environment. A new goal, a new route, a new image in his external environment attracts him and he deceives himself that achieving this new object of desire will bring him happiness and tranquility. This is an experience common to all.

People set up a goal that is based on social standards of status or personal gratification and spend all their effort and energy to achieve it, but when it is achieved, the gratification is momentary and the quest for happiness continues. This is because we are trying to adapt ourselves to the environment, which is ever changing and unstable. As soon as we reach a goal, our materialistic nature, which is unstable, has already changed to a new tune set by the external world. Thus, whatever energy is spent trying to build stability, tranquility, and absolute happiness based upon the unstable world is futile. In the midst of all these variables how can one reach contentment? An example which may explain this state of instability is that of a large body of water. If many outlets exist, the water is not contained. The water runs out aimlessly if there are no canals constructed to guide it, and soon the water is absorbed by the earth and the benefit of all this wealth is minimal. Soon this resource is wasted and the water is gone. The solution, we know, is constructing a dam. The same is true for human beings. Religion is the manual for constructing a spiritual dam to prevent the devastation, disintegration, and gradual dissipation of our energies and inner strength by our earthly attachments and external belongings. Just as constructing a dam prevents the waste of water, controlling the five senses, correctly practicing concentration and meditation, and learning to direct all energy using our resources in a focused manner, prevents the waste of our valuable time and capabilities. "And He loves those who keep themselves pure and clean." (*Holy Qur'an, 2:222*)

Concentration of energies and inner strength on one focal point has been the practice of true scientists throughout time, and has resulted in their various discoveries. True scientists and scholars are aware that it was neither the simple fact of a falling apple nor Newton's eyes perceiving the event that caused his cognition of the law of gravity. Rather it was focusing all his energies and thought processes on one point and his momentary placement of his true "self" with its infinite wisdom that opened his inner vision to the law of gravity. In that instant in which he resided in the state of true "self", a mere action unfolding its limited appearance allowed Newton's "self" to experience and recognize the magnificent and unlimited law, hidden beyond the superficial appearances. Obviously, if it were merely the event of an apple falling from a tree, or any other object or manifestation of nature that led to the cognition of the laws of existence, many others who see these or similar events would also discover the laws of nature. This is not the case, as we all know. Depending on the perceptions of the senses does not lead anyone to the path of discovery and cognition. Eyes see but have no vision; ears hear but have no auditory comprehension. As Jesus said, "Only those who have ears shall hear."

> "Whatever is seen outwardly and imagined inwardly is illusion,
> Whatever is witnessed through the heart and observed externally is truth."

A very significant part of the teachings of Sufism is purification. It is obvious that a balloon carrying sacks of sand would remain attached to earth and would be unable to rise and float in the skies above, as it is intended to do. The individual, who is attached to Earth by desires, jealousy, anger, hatred, and other cellular drives, cannot experience the boundless world within himself. Removal and separation from these attachments, and purification of one's identity from impurities results in freedom from the dense, harsh physical existence, so that one may enter the kingdom of spiritual existence - the state of tranquility and survival. This is why the Holy Prophet of Islam states:

> "Say: 'I am but a man like yourselves, (but) the inspiration has come to me, that your God is One God: Whoever expects to meet his Lord, let him work righteousness, and, in the worship of his Lord, admit no one as partner.'"[9]

One should ask himself, why is there neither revelation nor mystical inspiration for me? Why have I not experienced my metaphysical existence and realized the depth of my being? The answer was revealed in the above verse from the *Holy Qur'an*. Do you want to experience the same? Then, "...work righteousness." Cut your bondage to earth, discard all your attachments, your loads and acquisitions and be free of all else but He, so that you may admit no one into the worship of your Lord, "...admit no one as partner."

The oyster can only present the precious pearl hidden inside it after breaking through the shell. The delicate seedling blossoms from the seed only after the wooden exterior is split. Similarly, the various layers of physical attachments, cellular desires and materialistic accumulations must detach in order for one's inherent knowledge to present itself and grow to its infinite capacity.

One of the fundamental principles in the teachings of Maktab Tarighat Oveyssi Shahmaghsoudi is the center point of one's being, which is the recipient of divine revelations and metaphysical inspirations. We have heard of the different types of concentration. Some concentrate on the area of their navel while others concentrate on a point outside of themselves, or on repeating a word or a phrase. While different temporary results may be achieved in each of these practices, none of them are unlimited or permanent. It resembles accumulating one's wealth and storing it in a bag with a hole in it; before long all that was accumulated is lost again. Whether it is one's navel, brain cells, visual focus on a point on the wall, or repeating words or phrases, all of these are limited and devoid of spirituality. One should concentrate on the center point of one's being which results in the blossoming of the metaphysical being and the unveiling of the infinite absolute existence.

This center is called the Source of Life. It is located in the heart and is considered the basis for all spiritual experience, revelation and interaction with existence. This focal point contains man's unlimited, unbounded knowledge. Its first function is revealed in the third week of embryonic development. Before this phase, life is exhibited in purely cellular form, in a mass of undifferentiated cells called blastula. In the third week, the first electrical pulse of life from this node initiates life in its future differentiated human form. Soon, the heart, brain, and other organs are formed. This first pulse, and every other pulse thereafter, is in harmony with existence. Consider a lamp that is connected to the source of electricity through the plug. As long as the connection is undisturbed it presents electricity in its own form. Any time that lamp wants to benefit from this unlimited, boundless electricity, it must be plugged in to the socket. For the human being, that point of connection, that plug, is the Source of Life. That point is constantly in harmony and in touch with existence, and the physical body and its function is dependent on this harmonious connection. The Source of Life is meant to provide life not only in the physiological level but in the metaphysical level as well. The elevation of man to his spiritual levels, what the Prophets have called the heavens or the kingdom of heaven, is through this point – the Source of Life.

What is of essence in the teachings of the School of Islamic Sufism is that if a meaning is to be revealed to man, a discovery to be made, and the reality of entities and events to be experienced as they truly are, that truth must be discovered from within oneself. That is to say, they must be inwardly known and experienced. So that man, who exists and is not separate from existence, may discover the vast and infinite existence with in his own being. Before this phase, life is exhibited in a state purely separate from existence. If man discovers the reality of his own being, all other matters will be easily known as well. It is stated in the *Holy Qur'an* (4:59), "O ye who believe! Obey God, and obey the Apostle, and those charged with authority among you." What is considered in this verse is the totality, the source of all emanations – the Creator, God. For example, the sun is the cause and the source of the existence of the Earth and other planets who are its offspring. In whatever way or form life is manifested, it follows the laws that have emanated from the central source – the sun. These same laws govern the various evolutionary stages of life as it is manifested on Earth, from the particle to the human being. As long as each entity is submitted to these laws, it is able to continue its evolutionary journey of completion.

The above Holy verse indicates that God is the source of all emanations, and the Holy Prophet (the Apostle) is the one who has the capacity to receive revelation – without the interference of a personal will – from the central source. For example, the moon that is seen in the sky reflects light, but it is not the source of light. The reason it is luminous is because it is situated within the field of the sun, and is submitted to the laws governing it. If it were to be derailed from its position it would no longer be the moon as we know it. The existence of all things is contingent upon a central source. The Holy Prophet and his successors are as the moon; their being is in total submission to God and the laws of God. In other words, just as the moon is seen and is luminous because of its connection and submission to the Sun, the Prophet manifests in the same manner the light of God. The Holy Prophet's emphasis on freedom and on detachment from bonds rests on his personal conviction and experience of total annihilation in the Almighty God – the central source of all that exists. It is the return to the Origin which enables each human being to know and manifest his heavenly dimension.

What is significant in the teachings of Islam in general, and Sufism in particular, is the all-encompassing and vast central source of existence which has manifested all that exists in its varying forms and stages. All that is seen is rooted in a central source, called capability, which is infinite and abundant. If you consider the letter of the alphabet "*alif*" (ﺍ) in Arabic, you will see that it starts from one point. The "*alif*" represents the various stages of that point from where the "*alif*" started. The "*alif*" bears no resemblance to the point, yet all of its manifestations are rooted in the point.

The evolutionary course of a seed is an example that can provide insight into this topic. A seed that has the capacity for growth is planted in healthy soil. Planting of the seed is in itself an announcement of a journey that is to take place. In other words, the seed has inevitably accepted undergoing a process of evolution. Each stage during its various phases of growth - roots, stem, branches, leaves, flowers and fruit - while bearing no resemblance to the seed, is rooted in the knowledge within that seed. Each phase manifests two laws; the first is comprehensiveness, and the second is the capacity to accept and manifest the laws governing it. In conclusion, nothing could have taken place in each phase of growth had there not been that central point from which all evolved. Each one of the points in each phase of growth is at the extension of the seed or root and contains the same attributes. It makes no difference which of the points we look at, for each manifestation is a reflection of the expansive innate command which is hidden within it. Nothing can take place in any of these points of growth other than what is within its own innate nature. Should the connection be cut at any point during this process, its course of life would terminate.

To explain this process further, if we draw a perpendicular line and a horizontal line that intersect each other, the point of intersection can be considered as the location where the seed is placed in the soil. The process of growth downward and upward from the central point where the seed has been placed will show that each point along this longitudinal axis is anchored on this central point which has manifested this growth process - root and stem. Each point along this axis contains within it all the attributes that are manifested in the other phases of growth. Therefore, nothing but what is within that seed can be manifested at any point of its growth. The cause for all the manifestations that we see is the life force (command, creator) which is unseen (hidden) within the seed and commands all the phases of growth. When it follows its innate laws and is able to move through its phases of growth, then we can say that it is one and in harmony with its own innate "command" or "creator" hidden within it. The will of each point of growth is one with the will of the central source, the "command" or the "creator". If you visualize this growth process on the longitudinal axis as I have described, it will take the form of

"Alif Lam Mim" (الم).

Let us consider again the following verses from the Holy Qur'an:

> "Alif Lam Mim. This is the Book; In it is guidance sure, without doubt, those who fear God; Who believe in the Unseen, Are steadfast in prayer, And spend out of what We Have provided for them"

If we look closely at the above verses we will see that the same law is explained - that the hidden core of all forms of life is the "Unseen" which cannot be validated through any physical experimentation, but is evident in its manifestations. When the human being follows its innate "Command", or the "Creator", he will be able to manifest the knowledge hidden within him. The human being is a book whose knowledge can be known only if he is in harmony and submitted to the laws governing his being. He must rise (*ghiyam*) and endeavor, and do righteous deeds until his entire being becomes imbued with the knowledge inherent in his being.

The knowledge within oneself can manifest itself on the physical life journey, or it can manifest itself on other levels. The human being's capacity for manifesting this knowledge is infinite. What prevents the human being from knowing his divinity is his attachment to his earthly appetites and desires. Life is absolute and the human being is capable of manifesting the "Absolute" within him, provided he is in balance and harmony with the source of life governing his being. When the human being is in the state of balance, he manifests "Life", therefore, his actions are rooted in the Divine Command, and cannot be anything but righteous. If he is in the state of carnal self, he manifests nature, and he will be subject to the laws governing nature - assimilation, absorption and dispersion.

When the Holy Prophet said, *"la ilaha ill'Allah"* (لَا إِلَٰهَ إِلَّا ٱللَّٰه), the first *"la"* (لَا) announces negation of self which in essence is that eternal existence. It is in effect, the breaking of limitation in the unlimited Existence. When the human being exists in limitation which is his natural existence or *"Mim"* (م), his life-journey is within the boundaries of nature. He has the capacity for transcendence, but only manifests Life in the realm of nature. When his existence is founded upon "la", rises (ghiyam) from "la", and negates all earthly bonds, he is declaring Life in its absolute form. Through self-annihilation, which is the essence of submission, he is able to manifest his eternal existence.

The reality of "*Allah*"(الله) is related to annihilation. When the Holy Prophet Mohammad (pbuh) said "Allah", it indicated his own state of annihilation in the Absolute Existence, and therefore, what he said contained guidance. Amir al-Mo'menin Ali (peace be upon him) was close to the Holy Prophet, both physically and spiritually, and whatever the Holy Prophet said, Amir al-Mo'menin experienced, and it became reality for him, indicating that there was physical and spiritual harmony which arose from the depth of Amir al-Mo'menin's central source of existence.

The law of Islam is "la ilaha ill 'Allah". When each level of the human being rises (ghiyam) from the central source which is the life principle, it is a state of ascension for him. There are seven alifs within the word "la ilaha ill 'Allah", each representing a different stage in the creation of the human being. To journey through these seven stages, he must continuously be in a state of repentance which means total awareness or turning towards his centrality or the qiblah. When the human being journeys through the seven stages of his being, then he attains his divinity as "created in the image of God". When the body, the words and the heart are focused on and are founded upon the Source of Life, all actions reflect the state of true devotion. As it is stated in the *Holy Qur'an* (24:37):

"Men whom neither traffic nor merchandise can divert from the

remembrance of God." "All (the celestial bodies) swim along, each

in its rounded course." (*Holy Qur'an, 21:33*)

This is why in the teachings of Sufism it is essential that each

person make the journey to the source of life in order to discover

the reality of his being and his place in this extensive universe.

In *The Principles of Faghr and Sufism*, Molana Shah Maghsoud has

said:

> "The human being's experiential and cognitive (reflective) path must ultimately lead to a method and a way, that through inward discoveries and stabilizing óf mental faculties and energies, he will be able to guide himself to a point of stability and inward cognition, so that he may know the reality of objects, circumstances, and events. That is to say, developing a vision and knowledge that is so totally encompassing, that nothing remains unknown in his scope of knowledge. God, please show me the reality of things as they are.
>
> Therefore, recognizing this method of discovery, which is most crucial and at the same time the most direct method of recognition, in the sublime school of self-knowledge is considered as the essential goal for the seeker. In my opinion, the source of life in the heart, the commander and the foundation for the life activities and the mechanical aspects and the existence of the human being, has a more delicate and profound responsibility - to lift the boundaries and limitations created by the mind which prevent the discovery of the universe beyond, and the cause of events. This method should

open a special chapter in the scientific book of the world. Although the knowledge of this central source and its stages of cognition are inherent and ancient in the book of the human being, yet, they have not been the subject of inquiry and recognition except for the elevated and pure souls, who are but a few.[10"]

"Observation of results and presentations by the limited perceptions of the senses and imaginary deductions of the mind will not bring forth the essence of being. Only the heart and spiritual focal point can reveal the unbounded existence. It is through concentrating and recognizing all the infinite capabilities of the source of life that one can discover the absoluteness of the universe. In Sufism, the point of focus is the heart and its purification through the seven stages brings enlightenment and enrichment of the soul. The heart resembles a mirror which can reflect the light of truth once it is cleansed of the external dust that has covered it. As the Holy Prophet Mohammad (pbuh) has said, "Knowledge is not acquired through study, but it is a light that God shines in the heart of he whom He wills."[11]

For the cognition of reality, man, the essence of existence, the most delicate of creations and the reflection of the absolute, has capabilities and instruments as boundless as creation itself. At the elevated, pure level of enlightenment, he can witness all the aspirations and glories of existence. He must free himself of the limitations of the senses. Based on the fact that in physical research and experiments sensory perceptions are unreliable, and the accuracy of the brain's imagined deductions are questionable, it is most clear that in metaphysics the senses and brain cells cannot offer useful results, nor are they considered essential.

In *The Principles of Faghr and Sufism,* Hazrat Shah Maghsoud

states:

> "Limitation of the senses and imagination on the one
> hand, isolated thinking and sensory barriers on the other,
> have made the human being descend from his human
> and heavenly elevated rank and prevented him from
> attaining the state of permanence of his true personality
> in the absolute eternal; and natural desires and tendencies
> have replaced his gnostic and sublime acts of devotion.
> The bountiful capability which is supposed to be the
> architect of his cognition and personality, in tending to
> the sensory expectations and illogical perceptions sinks
> in the desert of his beastly appetites and material desires.
> The guidance of capability in its true and constructive
> course, is the journey of the personality in following
> the path of the caravan of the martyrs and lovers of
> Existence, those who have always guided thirsty souls
> to the final purpose and ultimate goal."[12]

In order to reach the ultimate level of knowledge, which is

recognizing the essence of existence and experiencing one's own

reality, it is clear that superficial observations and limited sensory

perceptions are not a suitable route to explore the essence of

knowledge, due to their limited potential.

Thus, Sufism emphasizes concentration of all powers and

energies in the heart. Harmony lies in repentance and purification

from earthly habits and attachments which separate man from

his inner self. When this harmony with existence is achieved in all physical and metaphysical levels, imaginary boundaries constructed by the mind collapse. Man then manifests himself in the unlimited horizon of existence and witnesses the unity of it. Only then will he know the meaning of *"la ilaha ill 'Allah"* - there is no other but God. Knowledge in its true meaning is the annihilation of the witness in the Witnessed, and the cognition of the unlimited after the boundaries of limitation have been lifted and the pure essence is manifest. Ocean mist can only find its essence when it is concentrated and appears in its original form of a droplet. Once it is concentrated into a drop, it still needs the guiding wind to direct it to the ocean. The instant the drop joins the ocean, it dissolves the limitation of physical appearance and all the forces of nature that cause its insignificant and limited form. It annihilates in the absolute reality of itself which is water, boundless and infinite as the ocean. So too it is essential for the seeker to pass through the stages of the journey from the limited to the unlimited, so that he can witness his own reality.

Since all the efforts of scientists through time have been to improve the condition of mankind, what could be more fruitful than the cognition of man himself? Only after man achieves his infinite wisdom and boundless capacity, and recognizes his true

potential, can he be of utmost benefit to himself and to others.

ENDNOTES

1. Angha, Molana al-Moazam Hazrat Shah Maghsoud Sadegh. (1989).
   Dawn. Lanham: University Press of America. p. 29.

2. Angha, Molana al-Moazam Hazrat Shah Maghsoud Sadegh. (1987).
   Principles of Faghr & Sufism. Verdugo City: M.T.O. Shahmaghsoudi
   Publications. p. 25.

3. Angha, Molana al-Moazam Hazrat Shah Maghsoud Sadegh. (1986). *Al-
   Rasa'el: The Light of Salvation.* Lanham: University Press of America. p. 80.

4. *From The World as I See It;* 1931.

5. *Principles of Faghr & Sufism.* p. 29.

6. Angha, Molana al-Moazam Hazrat Shah Maghsoud Sadegh. (1986).
   Manifestations of Thought. Verdugo City: M.T.O. Shahmaghsoudi
   Publications. p. 56.

7. *Nahj-ol Balaghah (The Teachings of Amir al-Mo'menin Ali):* translated
   by Haj Seyd Au Naghi Feyz-ol-Islam. Tehran: Entesharat Faghih, 1985.
   p. 215.

8. Angha, Molana al-Moazam Hazrat Mir Ghotbeddin Mohammad.
   (1986). *From Fetus to Paradise.* Verdugo City: M.T.O. Shahmaghsoudi
   Publications. p. 8.

9. *Nahj-ol Fissahah (The recorded teachings of the Holy Prophet Mohammad):*
   translated by Abolghassem Payandeh. Tehran: Sazman Entesharat
   Javidan, 1980. p. 102.

10. *Principles of Faghr & Sufism,* p. 95.

11. Angha, Molana al-Moazam Hazrat Shah Maghsoud Sadegh. (1986). *Al-
    Rasa'el: Al-Salat.* Lariham: University Press of America. p. 33.

12. *Principles of Faghr & Sufism,* p. 116.